Better Homes and Gardens®

2001 cross stitch designs

the essential reference book

Better Homes and Gardens® Books
An Imprint of Meredith® Books

Better Homes and Gardens® Books
An imprint of Meredith® Books

2001 Cross Stitch Designs

Editor: Carol Field Dahlstrom
Technical Editor: Susan Banker
Graphic Designer: Marisa Dirks
Copy Chief: Catherine Hamrick
Copy and Production Editor: Terri Fredrickson
Contributing Copy Editor: Jill Philby
Contributing Proofreader: Colleen Johnson
Photographer: Andy Lyons
Technical Illustrator: Chris Neubauer Graphics
Electronic Production Coordinator: Paula Forest
Editorial and Design Assistants: Judy Bailey, Kaye Chabot, Treesa Landry, Karen Schirm
Production Director: Douglas M. Johnston
Production Manager: Pam Kvitne
Assistant Prepress Manager: Marjorie J. Schenkelberg

Meredith® Books
Editor in Chief: James D. Blume
Design Director: Matt Strelecki
Managing Editor: Gregory H. Kayko

Director, Sales & Marketing, Retail: Michael A. Peterson
Director, Sales & Marketing, Special Markets: Rita McMullen
Director, Sales & Marketing, Home & Garden Center Channel: Ray Wolf
Director, Operations: George A. Susral

Vice President, General Manager: Jamie L. Martin

Better Homes and Gardens® Magazine
Editor in Chief: Jean LemMon

Meredith Publishing Group
President, Publishing Group: Christopher M. Little
Vice President, Consumer Marketing & Development: Hal Oringer

Meredith Corporation
President and Chief Executive Officer: William T. Kerr

Chairman of the Executive Committee: E. T. Meredith III

Cover photography: Andy Lyons

All of us at Better Homes and Gardens® Books are dedicated to providing you with information and ideas to create beautiful and useful projects. We welcome your comments and suggestions. Write to us at: Better Homes and Gardens® Books, Crafts Editorial Department, 1716 Locust St., Des Moines, IA 50309-3023.

If you would like to purchase any of our books, check wherever books are sold.

Permission to photocopy the patterns on *pages 314–329* for personal use is granted by Better Homes and Gardens® Books.

a treasury of cross-stitch

Welcome to this exciting and extensive collection of cross-stitch designs. We carefully chose hundreds of motifs representing every facet of life—holidays, children, nature, animals, sports, professions, and much more. Each collection of motifs is presented on an heirloom-quality reference plate and grouped by specific type so you'll be able to find your favorites quickly and easily. And beginning on *page 294*, we've added information about basic cross-stitch, tips on how to design your own work, 48 easy-to-follow specialty stitches—plus project patterns complete with detailed instructions.

We hope you think of *2001 Cross Stitch Designs* as an essential resource in your library and that you reach for it time and time again as you begin to stitch your treasured cross-stitch pieces.

Carol Field Dahlstrom

about this book

chapter one: florals

chapter two: for the little ones

chapter three: symbols of love

contents

chapter four: christmas fun

chapter five: santas and snowmen

chapter six: borders and patterns

chapter seven:
country patterns

chapter eight:
americana

chapter nine:
year-round holidays

chapter ten:
nature designs

chapter eleven:
animals

chapter twelve:
alphabets and numbers

chapter thirteen:
sports, professions, and pastimes

about this book...

Here it is—all in one book—a collection of 2001 designs along with specialty stitches, design helps, patterns, project ideas, and more.

Each chapter is filled with dozens (sometimes hundreds!) of motifs that fit each stitching category. We've grouped the designs on a vintage-style reference plate of similar-style designs (modeled after reference books of the 19th Century) and provided a color key that coordinates with each design plate. The plates are named and numbered for easy reference as well.

How can we think of so many designs? As stitchers and crafters we all are inspired by many things around us, and we've included a list of some of those inspirations. From nature to architecture, from the toys of childhood to the pride of our national flag, we give some of the secrets that inspired so many of these exquisite designs. Hopefully they may be the beginning of inspirations for you as well.

We've also listed idea after idea of how to use these motifs. How about stitching a border on your little girl's pinafore, or a design on your son's baseball cap? And there is always that time when you need a gift quickly. Try stitching a key chain and personalize it for that special friend. We have 2001 stitching motifs for you to choose from.

On *pages 302–305* we've given you tips and techniques for choosing and combining motifs and how to plan for some specific projects. We've even provided some patterns to get you started (see *pages 312–329*). And on *pages 306–311* we've compiled 48 beautiful specialty stitches for your reference. Finally, we've given you a detailed index so finding the right motif will be quick and easy.

So go ahead, be inspired with the designs and ideas we have given you in this book and begin using your stitching talents to create that perfect cross-stitch piece.

From elegant roses freshly picked from formal gardens to simple violets plucked from country flower beds, this collection of motifs is inspired by the beauty that only nature provides. This exquisite grouping of floral designs is organized by color and species so you can easily pick your favorite bloom to stitch. Hues from nature's extraordinary palette supply the color excitement in each of the designs in this section. Come stitch an everlasting bouquet.

florals

roses

inspirations
The breathtaking rose, the ultimate symbol of love and devotion, inspires our first cross-stitched plate that displays many varieties of this elegant flower.

ideas

- Stitch a border of roses along the hem of a curtain valance to add a romantic touch.
- Create a floral tablecloth by repeating one of the rose designs on each corner.
- Stitch one of the larger rose designs on perforated plastic, trim in a circular shape, and fill in the background with a solid color to make a lovely coaster.

plate no. 1
roses

roses

instruction

We stitched the Roses cross-stitch plate, *opposite*, over two threads on 28-count Wedgewood (#501) Lugana fabric. All cross-stitches are completed using two plies of cotton embroidery floss. All other stitches are completed using one ply of floss.

ROSES

ANCHOR		DMC
002	·	000 White
109	×	209 Lavender
1006	☆	304 Christmas red
010	○	351 Coral
1047	✳	402 Mahogany
231	:	453 Shell gray
267	□	470 Medium avocado
266	+	471 Light avocado
212	◉	561 Dark seafoam
210	◪	562 Medium seafoam
208	=	563 True seafoam
206	S	564 Light seafoam
936	◆	632 Cocoa
293	L	727 Topaz
259	⌃	772 Loden
307	⊕	783 Christmas gold
161	◉	813 Powder blue
271	⧄	819 Pink
1044	▲	895 Dark hunter green
052	♡	899 Rose
073	–	963 Rose pink
243	◇	988 Light forest green
242	⌐	989 Pale forest green
268	△	3346 Light hunter green
264	⊠	3347 Yellow green
059	♥	3350 Deep dusty rose
068	✳	3687 True mauve
060	⊡	3688 Medium mauve
049	⊿	3689 Light mauve
1016	‖	3727 Light antique mauve
076	⊞	3731 Dark dusty rose
869	∿	3743 Antique violet
1015	●	3777 Terra-cotta
305	◈	3821 Straw
363	I	3827 Golden brown

ANCHOR		DMC
BACKSTITCH		
109	╱	209 Lavender
307	╱	783 Christmas gold
380	╱	838 Beige brown
1044	╱	895 Dark hunter green
068	╱	3687 True mauve
1019	╱	3802 Deep antique mauve
STRAIGHT STITCH		
002	╱	000 White
307	╱	783 Christmas gold
380	╱	838 Beige brown
FRENCH KNOT		
010	○	351 Coral
380	●	838 Beige brown
305	○	3821 Straw

roses

yellows, golds, & white

inspirations
Fragrant lily of the valley, cheerful daisies, and towering sunflowers are some of the flowers that inspire this eclectic collection.

ideas

- Use waste canvas to stitch a bright yellow flower on the bib of denim overalls to adorn your gardening apparel.
- Stitch a single bloom on the front of a solid-color, baseball-style cap.
- Cut a picture-frame-shaped piece of perforated plastic and stitch a bloom in one corner. Fill in the background with black cross-stitches and add contrasting French knot polka dots to create a striking frame.

plate no. 2
yellows, golds, and white

yellows, golds, & white

instruction

We stitched the Yellows, Golds, and White cross-stitch plate, *opposite,* over two threads on 28-count Cameo Rose (#484) Cashel Linen fabric. All cross-stitches are completed using two plies of cotton embroidery floss. All other stitches are completed using one ply of floss.

YELLOWS, GOLDS, AND WHITE

ANCHOR		DMC
002	⊡	000 White
217	☒	367 Medium pistachio
214	▽	368 Light pistachio
231	◎	453 Shell gray
267	⊕	470 Medium avocado
266	⊟	471 Light avocado
878	▲	501 Dark blue green
877	☐	502 Medium blue green
1042	Ⅱ	504 Pale blue green
295	♡	726 Light topaz
293	Ⓢ	727 Pale topaz
302	☆	743 Yellow
275	⌃	746 Off-white
128	∟	775 Baby blue
359	◉	801 Medium coffee brown
218	◆	890 Deep pistachio
1033	⊞	932 True antique blue
269	⊠	937 Pine green
381	★	938 Deep coffee brown
1002	◇	977 Light golden brown
292	⠆	3078 Lemon
268	✳	3345 Hunter green
264	◈	3347 Yellow green
306	✥	3820 Dark straw
305	▨	3821 True straw
874	Ⅲ	3822 Light straw
1048	▶	3826 Dark golden brown

ANCHOR		DMC
BACKSTITCH		
267	╱	470 Medium avocado
877	╱	502 Medium blue green
1041	╱	844 Beaver gray
218	╱	890 Deep pistachio
1034	╱	931 Medium antique blue
381	╱	938 Deep coffee brown
306	╱	3820 Dark straw
1048	╱	3826 Dark golden brown
STRAIGHT STITCH		
1002	╱	977 Light golden brown
FRENCH KNOT		
275	●	746 Off-white
LAZY DAISY		
267	⬭	470 Medium avocado

yellows, golds, and white

pinks, reds, & oranges

inspirations
Red fuchsia plants, variegated pink tulips, and orange daylilies are just some of the blooms that inspire this vibrant pocketful of posies.

ideas

- Stitch a sprinkling of tiny flowers on a tea cozy.
- Make place mats by stitching a bloom in one corner of a solid-colored evenweave fabric mat.
- Chart and stitch the word, "Welcome," and surround it with favorite floral motifs (see the alphabets on *pages 242–279*).

plate no. 3
pinks, reds, and oranges

pinks, reds, & oranges

instruction

We stitched the Pinks, Reds, and Oranges cross-stitch plate, *opposite*, over two threads on 28-count Light Teal Green (#661) Annabelle fabric. All cross-stitches are completed using two plies of cotton embroidery floss. All other stitches are completed using one ply of floss.

FLORALS: PINKS, RED, ORANGES - D

ANCHOR		DMC	
002	⊡	000	White
352	◆	300	Mahogany
011	⊠	350	Medium coral
010	◎	351	Light coral
009	⊿	352	Pale coral
266	▽	471	Light avocado
253	⊟	472	Pale avocado
683	●	500	Blue-green
212	⊞	561	Dark seafoam
210	▣	562	Medium seafoam
208	☆	563	True seafoam
050	⌞	605	Cranberry
256	⊞	704	Chartreuse
088	♡	718	Plum
295	⊟	726	Topaz
169	◉	806	Dark peacock blue
023	⏽	818	Pink
257	⊖	905	Parrot green
076	★	961	Dark rose pink
075	⊕	962	Medium rose pink
1001	⊠	976	Golden brown
036	⟦S⟧	3326	Rose
268	▲	3345	Hunter green
266	△	3347	Yellow green
059	♥	3350	Dusty rose
086	▷	3608	Fuchsia
1028	◗	3685	Mauve
167	◇	3766	Light peacock blue
059	▼	3804	Dark cyclamen
062	⫴	3806	Light cyclamen
9575	⠒	3824	Melon
5975	◙	3830	Terra-cotta

ANCHOR		DMC	
BACKSTITCH			
683	╱	500	Blue-green – leaves, stems
013	╱	817	Deep coral – orange flowers
380	╱	838	Beige-brown – stems, flowers, flower centers, leaves
1028	╱	3685	Mauve – flowers
236	╱	3799	Charcoal – ribbons, flowers, flower stem, leaves
STRAIGHT STITCH			
256	╱	704	Chartreuse – stem
013	╱	817	Deep coral – center of hibiscus
1028	╱	3685	Mauve – flower center
9575	╱	3824	Melon – hibiscus center
LAZY DAISY			
683	⟋	500	Blue-green – leaves
380	⟋	838	Beige-brown – flower centers
FRENCH KNOT			
295	○	726	Topaz – flower centers
236	●	3799	Charcoal – flower center

pinks, reds, and oranges

containers

inspirations These lovely designs are inspired by both the expected and the unexpected places where flowers find a home—in a dainty antique teacup, a terra-cotta pot, a natural woven basket, a hanging planter, and a watering can.

ideas

- Make a lovely brooch by stitching any one of these motifs over one thread on a fine-weave linen.
- Create a garden-like border along the edging of a sheet or pillowcase.
- Trim a terra-cotta pot by repeating a small floral design on premade cross-stitch banding fabric.

plate no. 4
containers

containers

instruction

We stitched the Containers cross-stitch plate, *opposite*, over two threads on 28-count Lavender (#559) Lugana fabric. All cross-stitches are completed using two plies of cotton embroidery floss. All other stitches are completed using one ply of floss.

CONTAINERS

ANCHOR		DMC	
002	·	000	White
110	♦	208	Dark lavender
109	✕	209	Medium lavender
1049	▢	301	Mahogany
042	◉	309	Rose
215	☆	320	True pistachio
118	◎	340	Medium periwinkle
117	♡	341	Light periwinkle
1043	⁄	369	Pale pistachio
398	═	415	Pearl gray
1045	⊞	436	Dark tan
267	▲	469	Avocado
102	●	550	Violet
062	▣	603	Cranberry
936	✱	632	Cocoa
256	✚	704	Chartreuse
295	○	726	Light topaz
293	S	727	Pale topaz
890	◩	729	Old gold
885	L	739	Pale tan
128	△	775	Light baby blue
024	⏀	776	Pink
131	★	798	Dark Delft blue
136	⊕	799	Medium Delft blue
043	♥	815	Garnet
944	✦	869	Hazel
028	‖	893	Carnation
333	◆	900	Burnt orange
1003	◇	922	Copper
381	■	938	Coffee brown
244	✳	987	Medium forest green
242	⋀	989	Pale forest green
144	⊠	3325	True baby blue
268	◈	3345	Hunter green
260	◿	3364	Loden

ANCHOR		DMC	
BACKSTITCH			
110	╱	208	Dark lavender
042	╱	309	Rose
150	╱	336	Navy
267	╱	469	Avocado
102	╱	550	Violet
295	╱	726	Light topaz
890	╱	729	Old gold
043	╱	815	Garnet
944	╱	869	Hazel
1003	╱	922	Copper
381	╱	938	Coffee brown
242	╱	989	Pale forest green
268	╱	3345	Hunter green
STRAIGHT STITCH			
295	╱	726	Light topaz
FRENCH KNOT			
042	●	309	Rose
150	●	336	Navy
890	●	729	Old gold

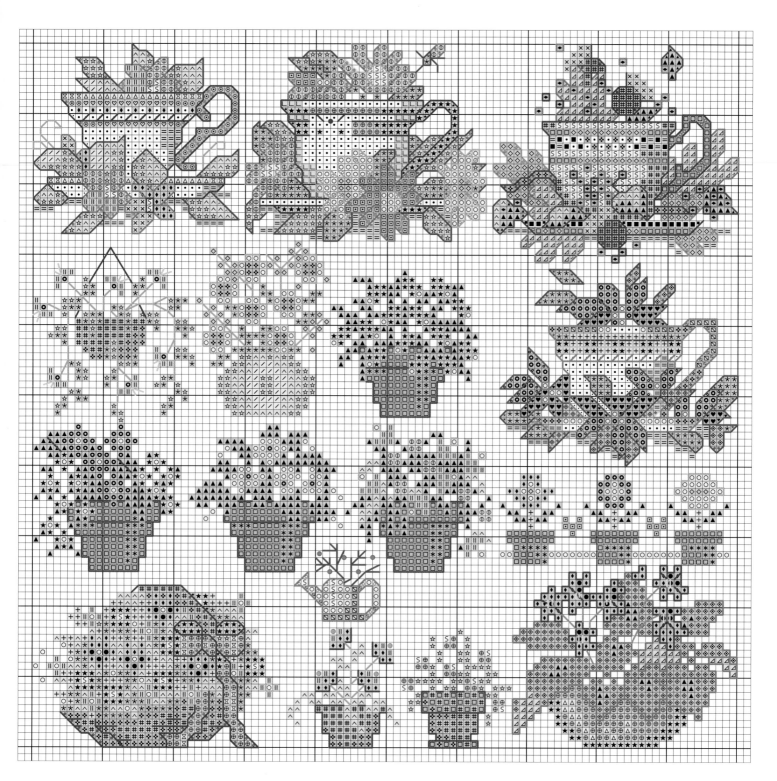

containers

lavender tones

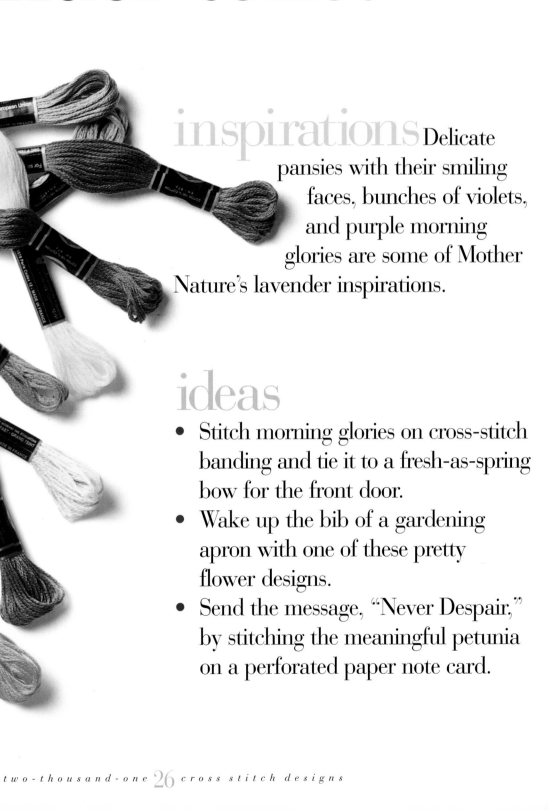

inspirations
Delicate pansies with their smiling faces, bunches of violets, and purple morning glories are some of Mother Nature's lavender inspirations.

ideas

- Stitch morning glories on cross-stitch banding and tie it to a fresh-as-spring bow for the front door.
- Wake up the bib of a gardening apron with one of these pretty flower designs.
- Send the message, "Never Despair," by stitching the meaningful petunia on a perforated paper note card.

plate no. 5
lavender tones

lavender tones

instruction

We stitched the Lavender Tones cross-stitch plate, *opposite,* over two threads on 28-count Ice Blue (#550) Jubilee fabric. All cross-stitches are completed using two plies of cotton embroidery floss. Blended needle stitches are worked using one ply of each color as listed in the key. All other stitches are completed using one ply of floss.

LAVENDER TONES

ANCHOR		DMC
002	⋅	000 White
110	⊞	208 Dark lavender
109	⊙	209 Medium lavender
342	⊟	211 Pale lavender
218	●	319 Pistachio
100	▧	327 Deep antique violet
117	◇	341 Light periwinkle
267	⊞	469 Dark avocado
266	⊚	470 Medium avocado
683	◆	500 Blue green
102	◆	550 Violet
210	✳	562 Seafoam
295	S	726 Light topaz
293	⧄	727 Pale topaz
303	∿	742 Tangerine
178	◣	791 Deep cornflower blue
177	⊖	792 Dark cornflower blue
906	⊞	829 Deep bronze
907	☆	833 Light bronze
256	△	906 Parrot green
204	□	913 Nile green
1003	★	922 Copper
189	◉	991 Dark aquamarine
187	▽	992 Medium aquamarine
292	⛉	3078 Lemon
268	▲	3345 Hunter green
264	⊟	3348 Yellow green
869	◻	3743 Pale antique violet
1030	⊕	3746 Dark periwinkle
176	☒	3807 True cornflower blue
305	▽	3821 Straw

ANCHOR		DMC
BACKSTITCH		
218	/	319 Pistachio
100	/	327 Deep antique violet
267	/	469 Dark avocado
178	/	791 Deep cornflower blue
906	/	829 Deep bronze
256	/	906 Parrot green
189	/	991 Dark aquamarine
236	/	3799 Charcoal
BLENDED BACKSTITCH		
256	/	906 Parrot green (1X) and
218		319 Pistachio (1X)
189	/	991 Dark aquamarine (1X) and
187		992 Medium aquamarine (1X)
STRAIGHT STITCH		
100	/	327 Deep antique violet
FRENCH KNOT		
303	●	742 Tangerine
1003	●	922 Copper
LAZY DAISY		
002	∅	000 White
267	∅	469 Dark avocado
178	∅	791 Deep cornflower blue
907	∅	833 Light bronze

lavender tones

flowers of the month

Looking past the garden gate to a bed of coral bells...a visit to a daffodil-filled greenhouse...colorful bouquets of carnations sent to a loved one—these floral pleasures inspire this garden of flowers that are selected to celebrate each month of the year.

ideas

- Stitch a personalized birthday greeting card for a special friend.
- Stitch the flowers in order horizontally, frame it, and hang the stitchery above the headboard for a garden-fresh addition to the bedroom.
- Select an appropriate afghan fabric to stitch these beautiful blooms upon.

plate no. 6
flowers of the month

(continued on *page 35*)

flowers of the month

instruction

We stitched the Flowers of the Month cross-stitch plate, *opposite*, over two threads on 28-count Ice Blue (#550) Jubilee fabric. All cross-stitches are completed using two plies of cotton embroidery floss. All other stitches are completed using one ply of floss unless otherwise noted in the key. The thick portion of the lettering can be achieved using either cross-stitches or vertical straight stitches. The flower design for December is on *page 37.*

FLOWERS OF THE MONTH

ANCHOR		DMC	
002	⊡	000	White
109	▨	209	Medium lavender
342	◿	211	Pale lavender
042	♥	309	Dark rose
100	▲	327	Antique violet
038	⊞	335	Medium rose
118	⊖	340	Medium periwinkle
117	◇	341	Light periwinkle
011	◉	350	Medium coral
009	▷	352	Pale coral
008	⊟	353	Peach
267	●	469	Dark avocado
266	⊟	471	Light avocado
098	✳	553	Violet
256	△	704	Chartreuse
324	▶	721	Bittersweet
295	▽	726	Topaz
279	☐	734	Olive
314	⊕	741	Tangerine
302	☆	743	Yellow
275	⦂	746	Off-white
307	◆	783	Christmas gold
258	◆	904	Deep parrot green
256	✕	906	Medium parrot green
1033	◎	932	True antique blue
073	◿	963	Rose pink
355	⌗	975	Golden brown
292	⊡	3078	Lemon
036	◎	3326	Pale rose
1030	◢	3746	Dark periwinkle
1031	⋈	3753	Pale antique blue

ANCHOR		DMC	
BACKSTITCH			
352	╱	300	Mahogany
042	╱	309	Dark rose
150	╱	336	Navy
359	╱	801	Coffee brown
045	╱	814	Garnet
1044	╱	895	Hunter green
256	╱	906	Medium parrot green (2X)
292	╱	3078	Lemon (2X)
STRAIGHT STITCH			
352	╱	300	Mahogany
FRENCH KNOT			
352	●	300	Mahogany
295	●	726	Topaz
359	●	801	Coffee brown
SATIN STITCH			
359	▥	801	Coffee brown

flowers of the month

(chart continued on *page 37*)

wildflowers

inspirations

Capture the glory of summer to enjoy any time of the year by stitching these floral designs. From vibrant daylilies sprinkled alongside a country road to old-fashioned bleeding hearts dancing around a vintage birdbath, this brilliant mix is inspired from nature's splendid creations.

ideas

- Dress up a plain-Jane blouse by stitching a flower on the collar or pocket.
- Use waste canvas to stitch a mini bouquet on a denim vest or jacket.
- Select your favorite flower to stitch on the corner of a purchased solid-color handkerchief.

plate no. 7
wildflowers

wildflowers

instruction

We stitched the Wildflowers cross-stitch plate, *opposite,* over two threads on 28-count Mushroom (#309) Lugana fabric. All cross-stitches are completed using two plies of cotton embroidery floss. Blended needle stitches are worked using one ply of each color floss as listed in the key. All other stitches are completed using one ply of floss. The chart with the Flowers of the Month for January through November is on *page 33.*

WILDFLOWERS

ANCHOR		DMC	
002	⊡	000	White
108	⊘	210	Lavender
352	◉	300	Mahogany
399	⑤	318	Steel
009	⊟	352	Coral
214	▽	368	Pistachio
373	⊞	422	Light hazel
266	◯	471	Light avocado
253	�captiveL	472	Pale avocado
862	▲	520	Olive drab
098	⊠	553	Violet
256	⊟	704	Chartreuse
305	☆	725	True topaz
295	⌃	726	Light topaz
275	⋮	746	Off-white
307	⊕	783	Christmas gold
045	♥	814	Dark garnet
944	◆	869	Dark hazel
381	■	938	Coffee brown
075	▣	962	Medium rose pink
1001	◎	976	Golden brown
244	⊠	987	Medium forest green
242	∿	989	Pale forest green
847	⊓	3072	Beaver gray
267	♡	3346	Hunter green
059	✳	3350	Dusty rose
025	◈	3716	Light rose pink
1031	Ⅲ	3753	Antique blue
1015	⋈	3777	Deep terra-cotta
5975	⌗	3830	True terra-cotta

ANCHOR		DMC	
BACKSTITCH			
002	╱	000	White
256	╱	704	Chartreuse
944	╱	869	Dark hazel
897	╱	902	Deep garnet
861	╱	934	Pine green
381	╱	938	Coffee brown
1001	╱	976	Golden brown
847	╱	3072	Beaver gray
267	╱	3346	Hunter green
059	╱	3350	Dusty rose
236	╱	3799	Charcoal
STRAIGHT STITCH			
305	╱	725	True topaz
861	╱	934	Pine green
BLENDED STRAIGHT STITCH			
305	╱	725	True topaz (1X) and
381		938	Coffee brown (1X)
FRENCH KNOT			
266	●	471	Light avocado
305	●	725	True topaz
LAZY DAISY			
002	⬮	000	White
897	⬮	902	Deep garnet

wildflowers

This collection of designs is sure to evoke happy smiles from the little ones in your life. Whether you are making a trim for a favorite pinafore, a curtain tie-back for a special nursery, or stitching a sampler of storybook characters to be treasured for a lifetime, this chapter provides you with many childlike pleasures. From teddy bears to fantasy figures, from bunnies to castles, each motif is especially designed to bring pleasure to you and yours.

for the little ones

kids, school, & toys

inspirations

From lovable dolls and colorful art supplies to miniature Noah's Ark creatures and fun boxes of all kinds, childhood favorites inspire this fun array of designs to stitch.

ideas

- Personalize a gym bag by stitching one (or several) of these whimsical designs on the bag using waste canvas.
- Use the chalkboard, lunch box, or stacked books designs to stitch a bookmark or paperweight for a teacher, tutor, or school nurse.
- Teach a child the art of cross-stitch by starting with one of the designs that requires few fractional stitches.

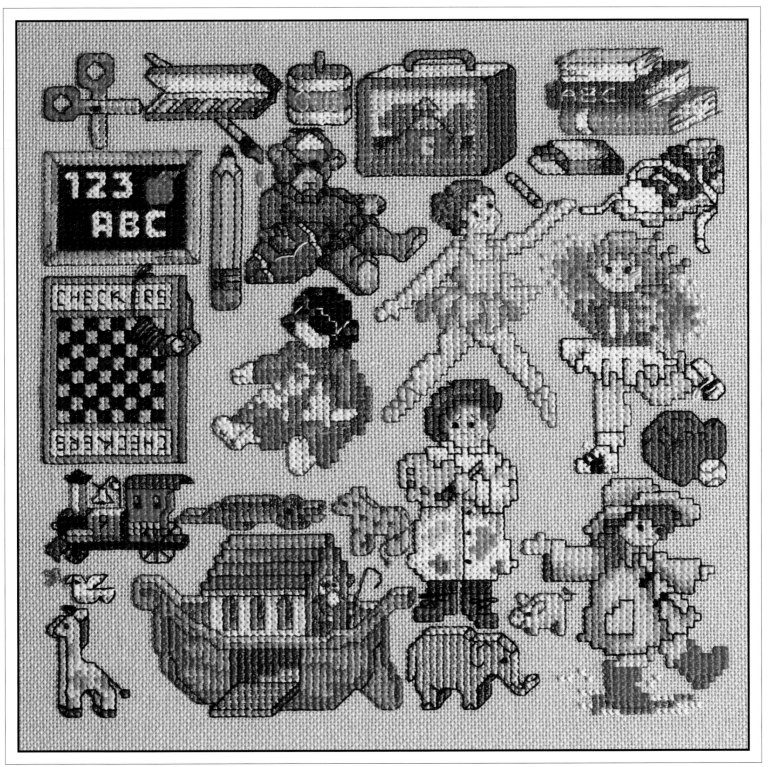

plate no. 8
kids, school, and toys

kids, school, & toys

instruction

We stitched the Kids, School, and Toys cross-stitch plate, *opposite,* over two threads on 28-count New Khaki (#307) Lugana fabric. All cross-stitches are completed using two plies of cotton embroidery floss. All other stitches are completed using one ply of floss.

KIDS, SCHOOL, AND TOYS

ANCHOR		DMC
002	⊡	000 White
895	◎	223 Medium shell pink
399	▢	318 Steel
218	◼	319 Pistachio
1025	◉	347 Salmon
401	▲	413 Pewter
398	◺	415 Pearl gray
1046	◙	435 Chestnut
362	◿	437 Medium tan
877	▤	502 Blue green
210	▨	562 Seafoam
886	⏸	677 Old gold
926	▯	712 Cream
295	▽	726 Light topaz
885	◠	739 Pale tan
314	☆	741 Medium tangerine
303	⊕	742 Light tangerine
1012	▭	754 Peach
882	▣	758 Terra-cotta
308	◆	782 Medium topaz
162	⬤	825 Dark bright blue
161	✕	826 Medium bright blue
379	⊖	840 Medium beige brown
033	⊞	892 Medium carnation
027	♡	894 Pale carnation
257	△	905 Dark parrot green
255	◠	907 Light parrot green
355	▦	975 Golden brown
896	♥	3721 Dark shell pink
140	◇	3755 Baby blue
1050	◩	3781 Mocha
306	✳	3820 Straw

ANCHOR		DMC
BACKSTITCH		
002	╱	000 White
403	╱	310 Black
303	╱	742 Light tangerine
043	╱	815 Garnet
162	╱	825 Dark bright blue
380	╱	838 Deep beige brown
027	╱	894 Pale carnation
257	╱	905 Dark parrot green
FRENCH KNOT		
002	●	000 White
403	●	310 Black
043	●	815 Medium garnet
380	●	838 Deep beige brown
LAZY DAISY		
002	⬭	000 White
403	⬭	310 Black
043	⬭	815 Garnet
257	⬭	905 Dark parrot green

kids, school, and toys

pretend

inspirations
Fanciful dragons, tiny fairies, and other magical motifs from fairy and folk tales inspire these fun-loving designs that are destined to spark the imagination in all of us.

ideas

- Make a pocket-shaped tooth-fairy pouch by stitching one of the fairies on the flap.
- Use small-count waste canvas to stitch an assortment of these characters on a child's sweatshirt.
- Stitch the sun and moon designs on a dark-colored afghan fabric.

plate no. 9
pretend

pretend

instruction

We stitched the Pretend cross-stitch plate, *opposite*, over two threads on 28-count Blueberry (#547) Annabelle fabric. All cross-stitches are completed with two plies of cotton embroidery floss or metallic thread. All other stitches are completed using one ply of floss, unless otherwise noted in the key.

PRETEND

ANCHOR		DMC	
002	⊡	000	White
110	◆	208	Dark lavender
109	⊠	209	Medium lavender
1006	♥	304	Christmas red
351	▼	400	Mahogany
055	♡	604	Light cranberry
891	⊟	676	Light old gold
886	S	677	Pale old gold
324	⊙	721	Medium bittersweet
323	⊞	722	Light bittersweet
305	▽	725	Topaz
890	▢	729	Medium old gold
303	⋀	742	Tangerine
1012	⋮	754	Peach
175	◇	794	Cornflower blue
258	▲	904	Deep parrot green
256	⊕	906	Medium parrot green
381	■	938	Coffee brown
187	⊞	958	True aqua
185	○	964	Light aqua
1001	⊠	976	Medium golden brown
189	★	991	Aquamarine
036	⧄	3326	Rose
035	☆	3705	Watermelon
120	⌴	3747	Periwinkle
059	⋈	3804	Dark cyclamen
062	▽	3806	Light cyclamen
1048	◉	3826	Dark golden brown
	‖	282Z	DMC Gold metallic embroidery thread
	⊟	283Z	DMC Silver metallic embroidery thread

ANCHOR		DMC	
BACKSTITCH			
351	╱	400	Mahogany
324	╱	721	Medium bittersweet
897	╱	902	Garnet
258	╱	904	Deep parrot green
152	╱	939	Navy
1001	╱	976	Medium golden brown
	╱	282Z	DMC Gold metallic embroidery thread (2X)
	╱	283Z	DMC Silver metallic embroidery thread (2X)
STRAIGHT STITCH			
110	╱	208	Dark lavender
050	╱	605	Pale cranberry
305	╱	725	Topaz
FRENCH KNOT			
002	●	000	White
324	●	721	Medium bittersweet
305	○	725	Topaz
303	●	742	Tangerine
897	●	902	Garnet
152	●	939	Navy
	●	282Z	DMC Gold metallic embroidery thread (2X)
	●	283Z	DMC Silver metallic embroidery thread (2X)
SMYRNA CROSS-STITCH			
050	✳	605	Pale cranberry
	✳	283Z	DMC Silver metallic embroidery thread (2X)
STAR STITCH			
	✳	283Z	DMC Silver metallic embroidery thread (2X)

pretend

baby motifs

inspirations

Oh-so-soft toys, fun carriage rides, and baby's play time inspire these delightful designs to cross-stitch with love.

ideas

- Make a mobile to hang above baby's crib by stitching a few of the larger designs on plastic canvas and backing them with bright felts.
- Trim a scarf for baby's dresser by using waste canvas to stitch the design.
- Surprise your little girl by stitching the mini motifs on some of her doll's clothes.

plate no. 10
baby motifs

baby motifs

instruction

We stitched the Baby Motifs cross-stitch plate, *opposite*, over two threads on 28-count Wedgewood (#501) Lugana fabric. All cross-stitches are completed with two plies of cotton embroidery floss. All other stitches are completed using one ply of floss.

BABY MOTIFS

ANCHOR		DMC	
002	▪	000	White
110	◆	208	Dark lavender
109	✕	209	Medium lavender
310	⊞	434	Chestnut
1045	◯	436	Dark tan
232	◻	452	Medium shell gray
231	◿	453	Light shell gray
324	☆	721	Bittersweet
885	⊟	739	Pale tan
303	▽	742	Tangerine
1012	⊟	754	Peach
133	▲	796	Royal blue
160	⋀	827	Powder blue
027	∟	894	Carnation
256	⊕	906	Parrot green
381	■	938	Coffee brown
297	⊠	973	Canary
433	ⓘ	996	Electric blue
035	♥	3705	Watermelon
025	◇	3716	Rose pink
1013	✳	3778	Terra-cotta

ANCHOR		DMC	
BACKSTITCH			
401	╱	413	Pewter
133	╱	796	Royal blue
256	╱	906	Parrot green
355	╱	975	Golden brown
433	╱	996	Electric blue
905	╱	3021	Brown gray
035	╱	3705	Watermelon
STRAIGHT STITCH			
401	╱	413	Pewter
303	╱	742	Tangerine
133	╱	796	Royal blue
433	╱	996	Electric blue
035	╱	3705	Watermelon
FRENCH KNOT			
401	●	413	Pewter
303	●	742	Tangerine
027	●	894	Carnation
355	●	975	Golden brown
905	●	3021	Brown gray
035	●	3705	Watermelon
LAZY DAISY			
110	✇	208	Dark lavender
303	✇	742	Tangerine
433	✇	996	Electric blue
035	✇	3705	Watermelon

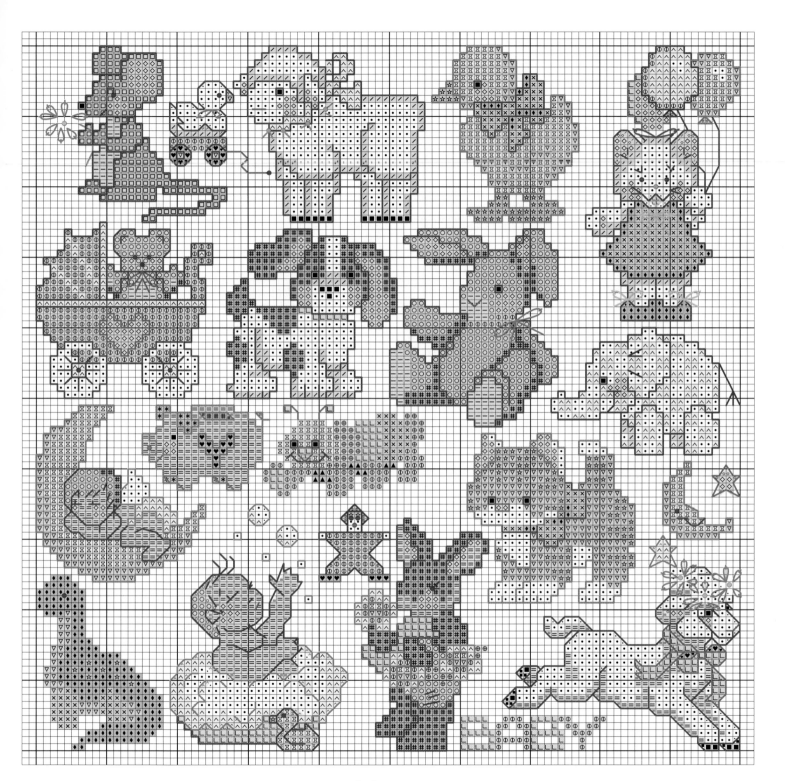

baby motifs

baby toys

inspirations Perfect for adorning baby's clothes or accessories, these playful designs are inspired by treasured toys and trinkets.

ideas

- Make bedtime fun by stitching a pastel pal on the front of baby's pajamas.
- Make curtain tie-backs by stitching the larger designs on plastic canvas using yarn.
- Create a baby shower card that will be saved for a lifetime by stitching one of these dear characters on perforated paper.

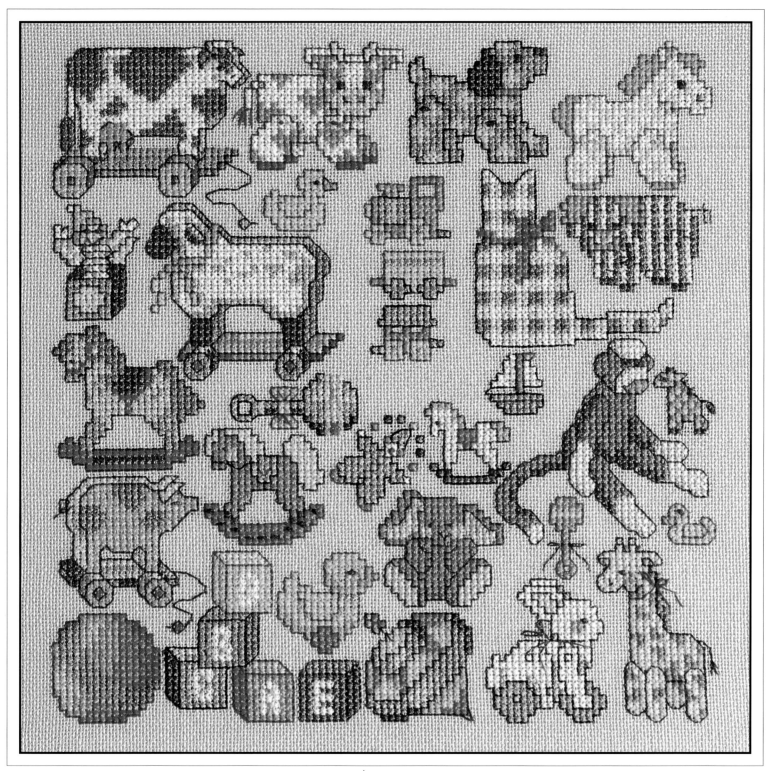

plate no. 11
baby toys

baby toys

instruction

We stitched the Baby Toys cross-stitch plate, *opposite*, over two threads on 28-count Lavender (#559) Lugana fabric. All cross-stitches are completed with two plies of cotton embroidery floss. All other stitches are completed using one ply of floss.

BABY TOYS

ANCHOR		DMC
002	⊡	000 White
119	▲	333 Deep periwinkle
118	⊠	340 Medium periwinkle
1025	◉	347 Salmon
235	◆	414 Steel
398	▽	415 Pearl gray
1046	⊞	435 Chestnut
162	★	517 Wedgwood blue
057	♥	601 Dark cranberry
062	◻	603 True cranberry
055	▤	604 Light cranberry
226	◇	702 Christmas green
238	⊕	703 True chartreuse
256	⌃	704 Light chartreuse
295	○	726 Light topaz
293	⌐	727 Pale topaz
885	⑤	739 Tan
314	☆	741 Tangerine
275	⟋	746 Off-white
1012	▬	754 Peach
882	♡	758 Terra-cotta
144	⫶	800 Delft blue
161	◎	813 Powder blue
379	△	840 Medium beige brown
206	∾	955 Nile green
035	⊞	3705 Dark watermelon
033	⊠	3706 Medium watermelon
031	⊿	3708 Light watermelon
1030	◗	3746 Dark periwinkle
1050	■	3781 Mocha
306	✳	3820 Straw

ANCHOR		DMC
BACKSTITCH		
002	╱	000 White
218	╱	319 Pistachio
119	╱	333 Deep periwinkle
150	╱	336 Navy
162	╱	517 Wedgwood blue
1005	╱	816 Garnet
380	╱	838 Deep beige brown
355	╱	975 Golden brown
FRENCH KNOT		
119	●	333 Deep periwinkle
150	●	336 Navy
055	●	604 Light cranberry
314	●	741 Tangerine
1005	●	816 Garnet
380	●	838 Deep beige brown
LAZY DAISY		
119	⊘	333 Deep periwinkle
162	⊘	517 Wedgwood blue
1005	⊘	816 Garnet

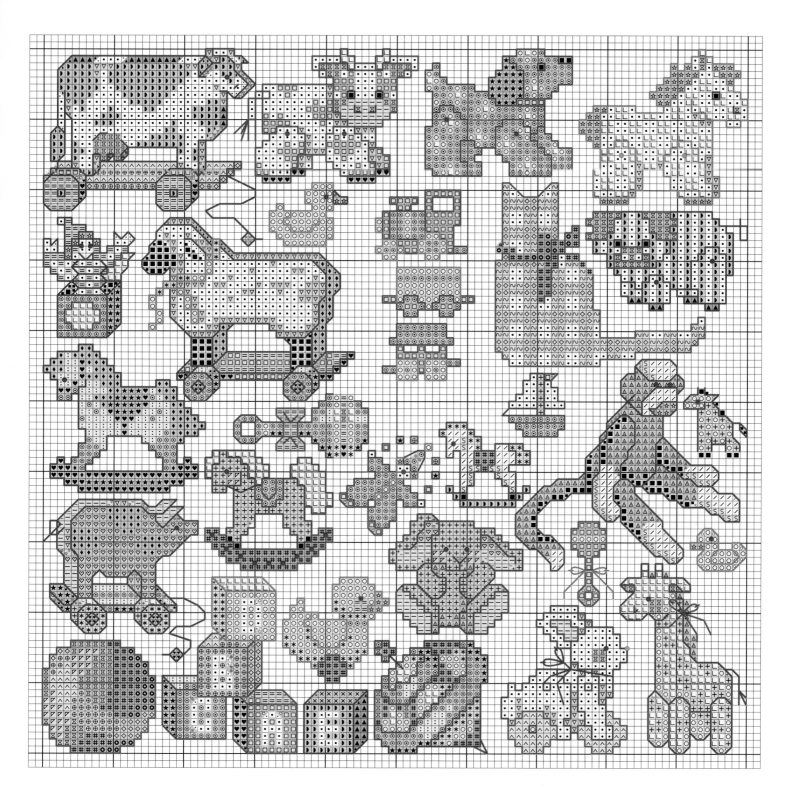

baby toys

mother goose

inspirations Beloved nursery rhymes, complete with their unforgettable characters, inspire this adorable collection.

ideas

- Design a baby sampler by combining favorite Mother Goose motifs (see the alphabets on *pages 242–279*).
- Adorn a baby bib in an evening using one of these precious designs.
- Stitch the Three Blind Mice or The Dish and The Spoon on the cuffs of tiny socks for a newborn.

plate no. 12
mother goose

mother goose

instruction

We stitched the Mother Goose cross-stitch plate, *opposite*, over two threads on 28-count Carnation Pink (#400) Jubilee fabric. All cross-stitches are completed using two plies of cotton embroidery floss. All other stitches are completed using one ply of floss.

MOTHER GOOSE

ANCHOR		DMC
002	⊡	000 White
289	▽	307 True lemon
1017	⊟	316 Antique mauve
399	⧈	318 Steel
008	♡	353 Peach
401	⧓	413 Pewter
398	∾	415 Pearl gray
358	◙	433 Dark chestnut
362	◸	437 Tan
290	⊛	444 Medium lemon
288	⧄	445 Light lemon
323	△	722 Bittersweet
300	☆	745 Light yellow
275	⎅	746 Off-white
024	⧅	776 Pink
161	⊠	813 Medium powder blue
162	●	826 Bright blue
160	◇	827 Light powder blue
380	▲	838 Beige brown
338	⊙	921 Copper
381	♦	938 Coffee brown
881	⊖	945 Ivory
054	⊞	956 Medium geranium
050	○	957 Light geranium
189	◆	991 Aquamarine
086	⊕	3608 Fuchsia
1030	⊖	3746 Periwinkle
1008	D	3773 Rose beige

ANCHOR		DMC
BACKSTITCH		
042	/	309 Rose
401	/	413 Pewter
1046	/	435 Light chestnut
323	/	722 Bittersweet
307	/	783 Christmas gold
381	/	938 Coffee brown
189	/	991 Aquamarine
779	/	3809 Turquoise
STRAIGHT STITCH		
002	/	000 White
FRENCH KNOT		
002	○	000 White
042	●	309 Rose
401	●	413 Pewter
307	●	783 Christmas gold
381	●	938 Coffee brown
054	●	956 Medium geranium
779	●	3809 Turquoise
LAZY DAISY		
189	0	991 Aquamarine
779	0	3809 Turquoise

mother goose

teddy bears

inspirations
One of the most adored toys of all times, the huggable teddy bear, is the friendly inspiration for this cuddly collection.

ideas

- Stitch and frame several of these furry pals separately to hang in a wall grouping.
- To make a perfect accessory for the nursery, stitch "Shhh...baby's sleeping" by the bear in the heart motif (see the alphabets on *pages 242–279*).
- Use waste canvas to add these terrific teddies to a soft baby blanket.

plate no. 13
teddy bears

teddy bears

instruction

We stitched the Teddy Bears cross-stitch plate, *opposite*, over two threads on 28-count Dutch Blue (#511) Cashel Linen fabric. All cross-stitches are completed using two plies of cotton embroidery floss. All other stitches are completed using one ply of floss.

TEDDY BEARS

ANCHOR		DMC	
002	·	000	White
403	■	310	Black
373	◿	422	Light hazel
358	◪	433	Dark chestnut
310	◩	434	Medium chestnut
1046	⊞	435	Light chestnut
1045	△	436	Dark tan
362	◻	437	Medium tan
933	◹	543	Pale beige brown
891	◿	676	Light old gold
238	▽	703	Chartreuse
295	☆	726	Topaz
890	◉	729	Medium old gold
361	▯	738	Light tan
359	▲	801	Coffee brown
168	⊙	807	Medium peacock blue
906	◆	829	Bronze
379	⊖	840	Medium beige brown
378	▢	841	True beige brown
388	◠	842	Light beige brown
258	◗	904	Parrot green
054	⊕	956	Medium geranium
050	♡	957	Light geranium
073	–	963	Rose pink
355	◎	975	Deep golden brown
905	◐	3021	Brown gray
167	◇	3766	Light peacock blue
1050	⊞	3781	Mocha
1048	☒	3826	Dark golden brown
363	⊟	3827	Pale golden brown
373	◿	3828	True hazel
890	✳	3829	Deep old gold

ANCHOR		DMC	
BACKSTITCH			
042	╱	309	Rose
310	╱	434	Medium chestnut
169	╱	806	Dark peacock blue
168	╱	807	Medium peacock blue
258	╱	904	Parrot green
054	╱	956	Medium geranium
382	╱	3371	Black brown
236	╱	3799	Charcoal
890	╱	3829	Deep old gold
STRAIGHT STITCH			
238	╱	703	Chartreuse
FRENCH KNOT			
403	●	310	Black
168	●	807	Medium peacock blue
054	●	956	Medium geranium
050	●	957	Light geranium
382	●	3371	Black brown
LAZY DAISY			
042	⟡	309	Rose
168	⟡	807	Medium peacock blue

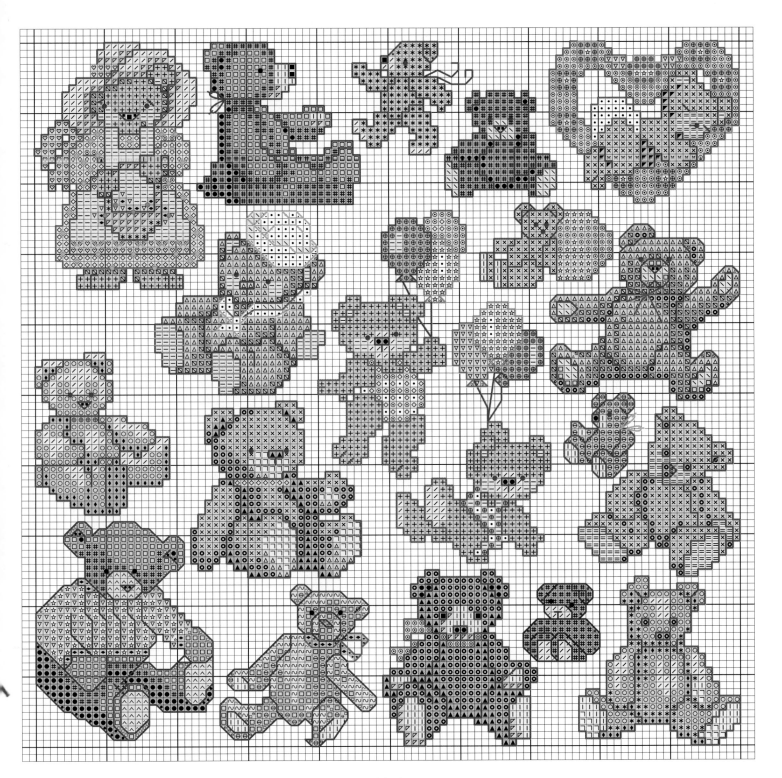

teddy bears

fun stuff

inspirations

Dinosaurs, clowns, carousel horses, fire engines, and more— things that capture a child's imagination and evoke ear-to-ear grins, inspire these bright fun-to-stitch designs.

ideas

- Transform an everyday T-shirt by stitching one of these playful designs on the front using small-count waste canvas.
- Adorn a child's book tote with a tug boat or dancing kitty (see the alphabets on *pages 242-279* to personalize the bag).
- Stitch a small motif at the top of a strip of perforated paper or plastic to make a bookmark.

plate no. 14
fun stuff

fun stuff

instruction

We stitched the Fun Stuff cross-stitch plate, *opposite*, over two threads on 28-count Mint Green (#621) Jubilee fabric. All cross-stitches are completed using two plies of cotton embroidery floss. All other stitches are completed using one ply of floss.

FUN STUFF

ANCHOR		DMC
002	·	000 White
108	⊘	210 Lavender
289	▽	307 True lemon
399	◇	318 Steel
9046	◉	321 Christmas red
119	◆	333 Periwinkle
401	⊞	413 Pewter
398	◺	415 Pearl gray
1045	□	436 Tan
290	☆	444 Medium lemon
055	○	604 Light cranberry
050	−	605 Pale cranberry
256	△	704 Chartreuse
314	⊕	741 Tangerine
310	◉	780 Topaz
144	Ι	800 Delft blue
162	●	825 Bright blue
209	⊖	912 Light emerald
340	▲	920 Copper
433	⊠	996 Electric blue
035	▷	3705 Watermelon
062	+	3806 Cyclamen
306	✳	3820 Straw

ANCHOR		DMC
BACKSTITCH		
002	/	000 White
401	/	413 Pewter
398	/	415 Pearl gray
290	/	444 Medium lemon
045	/	814 Garnet
162	/	825 Bright blue
905	/	3021 Brown gray
236	/	3799 Charcoal
062	/	3806 Cyclamen
923	/	3818 Deep emerald
STRAIGHT STITCH		
002	/	000 White
289	/	307 True lemon
309	/	781 Dark topaz
FRENCH KNOT		
9046	●	321 Christmas red
290	○	444 Medium lemon
045	●	814 Garnet
433	●	996 Electric blue
905	●	3021 Brown gray
236	●	3799 Charcoal
306	○	3820 Straw
ALGERIAN EYELET VARIATION		
256	✴	704 Chartreuse
LAZY DAISY		
062	✐	3806 Cyclamen

fun stuff

Filled with heartwarming and sentimental notions, this chapter offers lovely designs to celebrate love and togetherness. Create valentines, gift tags, samplers, and more by using a single motif or combining a few of your favorites. Whether you stitch a delicate blossom, a filagree heart, or a miniature wedding cake for the happy bride and groom, a gift from this heartfelt collection will be treasured for a lifetime.

symbols of love

weddings & anniversaries

inspirations
To honor marriage, these precious designs are inspired by wedding-day traditions and include motifs to help celebrate wedding anniversaries for years to come.

ideas

- Create a beautiful pillow for the ring bearer to carry by combining a few designs.
- Make a lovely wedding cake topper by stitching the bells and roses design on perforated plastic and attach it to the center of a ribbon bow.
- Design an unforgettable anniversary sampler for friends (see the alphabets on *pages 242–279*).

weddings & anniversaries

instruction

We stitched the Weddings and Anniversaries cross-stitch plate, *opposite,* over two threads on 28-count Ice Blue (#550) Lugana fabric. All cross-stitches are completed with two plies of cotton embroidery floss. All other stitches are completed using one ply of floss.

WEDDINGS AND ANNIVERSARIES

ANCHOR		DMC
002	·	000 White
342	∾	211 Lavender
400	⊞	317 Pewter
1046	◆	435 Chestnut
210	◗	562 Seafoam
273	◉	645 Dark beaver gray
1040	▢	647 True beaver gray
900	◣	648 Light beaver gray
256	△	704 Chartreuse
293	╱	727 Topaz
024	○	776 Pink
131	●	798 Delft blue
359	◎	801 Coffee brown
052	⊞	899 Rose
4146	▭	950 Rose beige
954	◩	954 Nile green
059	♥	3350 Dusty rose
167	◇	3766 Peacock blue
236	▲	3799 Charcoal
168	☒	3810 Turquoise
306	✳	3820 Dark straw
874	▽	3822 Light straw
396	▯	3823 Yellow

ANCHOR		DMC
BACKSTITCH		
002	╱	000 White
1046	╱	435 Chestnut
273	╱	645 Dark beaver gray
131	╱	798 Delft blue
359	╱	801 Coffee brown
045	╱	814 Garnet
218	╱	890 Pistachio
052	╱	899 Rose
236	╱	3799 Charcoal
874	╱	3822 Light straw
STRAIGHT STITCH		
002	╱	000 White
256	╱	704 Chartreuse
052	╱	899 Rose
FRENCH KNOT		
002	●	000 White
273	●	645 Dark beaver gray
024	○	776 Pink
131	●	798 Delft blue
359	●	801 Coffee brown
045	●	814 Garnet
052	●	899 Rose
4146	○	950 Rose beige
236	●	3799 Charcoal
874	○	3822 Light straw
LAZY DAISY		
273	⊘	645 Dark beaver gray
256	⊘	704 Chartreuse
052	⊘	899 Rose

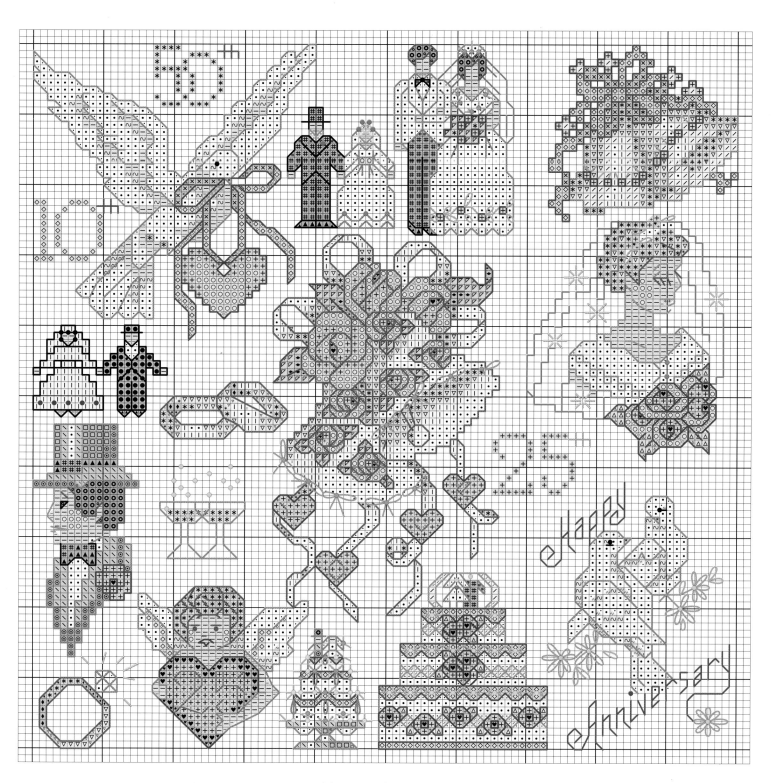

weddings and anniversaries

hearts & flowers (a

Country checkerboards, vintage linens, emotion-packed Valentines, and arrows of love inspire this charming collection of pastel hearts.

ideas

- Welcome company by stitching a band of hearts on guest towels.
- To make clever button covers, stitch a small heart motif to cover a button form.
- Stitch a row of hearts across the hem of a little one's pinafore.

plate no. 16
hearts and flowers (a)

hearts & flowers (a)

instruction

We stitched the Hearts and Flowers (A) cross-stitch plate, *opposite*, over two threads on 28-count Mint Green (#621) Jubilee fabric. All cross-stitches are completed with two plies of cotton embroidery floss. All other stitches are completed using one ply of floss.

HEARTS AND FLOWERS (A)

ANCHOR		DMC	
002	⊡	000	White
119	◆	333	Deep periwinkle
977	◎	334	Dark baby blue
118	⊠	340	Medium periwinkle
013	♥	349	Dark coral
011	▢	350	Medium coral
010	⊞	351	Light coral
009	◪	352	Pale coral
008	⊞	353	Peach
933	⠒	543	Beige brown
210	◉	562	Medium seafoam
208	✳	563	True seafoam
055	▽	604	Cranberry
891	◇	676	Old gold
300	⊟	745	Yellow
259	⫿	772	Loden
308	☆	782	Topaz
132	△	797	Royal blue
131	★	798	Delft blue
076	✤	961	Dark rose pink
073	∟	963	Pale rose pink
246	▲	986	Dark forest green
242	♡	989	Pale forest green
1030	⊕	3746	Dark periwinkle
140	⊠	3755	Medium baby blue
063	◈	3805	True cyclamen
305	⊕	3821	Straw

ANCHOR		DMC	
BACKSTITCH			
002	╱	000	White
119	╱	333	Deep periwinkle
977	╱	334	Dark baby blue
210	╱	562	Medium seafoam
055	╱	604	Cranberry
308	╱	782	Topaz
132	╱	797	Royal blue
043	╱	815	Garnet
076	╱	961	Dark rose pink
246	╱	986	Dark forest green
242	╱	989	Pale forest green
059	╱	3350	Dusty rose
236	╱	3799	Charcoal
063	╱	3805	Cyclamen
FRENCH KNOT			
002	●	000	White
308	●	782	Topaz
246	●	986	Dark forest green
059	●	3350	Dusty rose
LAZY DAISY			
308	⌒	782	Topaz
COUCHING			
002	╱	000	White couched with
305		3821	Straw

hearts and flowers (a)

hearts & flowers (b

inspirations

This delicate plate is inspired by elegant flowers and romantic hearts of all sizes and shapes—symbols that instantly say, "I love you."

ideas

- Stitch pastel hearts as a border around a bread cloth for a Valentine's Day dinner.
- Stitch a tiny heart in the corner of a linen handkerchief for a bride to carry on her wedding day.
- Make a romantic pillow, by stitching this entire plate and finishing the pillow edges with a satin ruffle.

plate no. 17
hearts and flowers (b)

hearts & flowers (b)

instruction

We stitched the Hearts and Flowers (B) cross-stitch plate, *opposite*, over two threads on 28-count Carnation Pink (#400) Jubilee fabric. All cross-stitches are completed using two plies of cotton embroidery floss. All other stitches are completed using one ply of floss.

HEARTS AND FLOWERS (B)

ANCHOR		DMC	
002	·	000	White
110	⊠	208	Dark lavender
108	⊟	210	Light lavender
978	△	322	Pale navy
102	◆	550	Deep violet
210	⊙	562	Medium seafoam
206	✳	564	Light seafoam
050	▽	605	Cranberry
256			704	Chartreuse
305	◇	725	True topaz
307	✱	783	Christmas gold
132	★	797	Royal blue
130	◉	809	Delft blue
257	▲	905	Parrot green
203	♡	954	Nile green
292	⊟	3078	Lemon
087	✤	3607	Dark fuchsia
086	⊕	3608	Medium fuchsia
085	◺	3609	Light fuchsia
1023	⊞	3712	Salmon
062	⊞	3806	Cyclamen

ANCHOR		DMC	
BACKSTITCH			
148	╱	311	True navy
978	╱	322	Pale navy
102	╱	550	Deep violet
098	╱	553	Medium violet
212	╱	561	Dark seafoam
210	╱	562	Medium seafoam
310	╱	780	Deep topaz
307	╱	783	Christmas gold
060	╱	3688	Medium mauve
069	╱	3803	Dark mauve
FRENCH KNOT			
002	●	000	White
212	●	561	Dark seafoam
305	○	725	True topaz
069	●	3803	Dark mauve
LAZY DAISY			
210	⬭	562	Medium seafoam

hearts and flowers (b)

valentines

inspirations

Flowers, hearts, Cupids, and lovebirds—these symbols send a message of love and are the inspiration for these cherished cross-stitch designs.

ideas

- Stitch your sweetheart a one-of-a-kind card for Valentine's Day.
- Stitch one of the heart motifs on the front of a toddler's romper or bib.
- Use waste canvas to stitch a heart on the cuff of a sock.

plate no. 18
valentines

valentines

instruction

We stitched the Valentines cross-stitch plate, *opposite*, over two threads on 28-count Bone (#253) Lugana fabric. All cross-stitches are completed using two plies of cotton embroidery floss. All other stitches are completed using one ply of floss, unless otherwise noted in the key.

VALENTINES

ANCHOR		DMC	
387	☑		Ecru
002	•	000	White
108	⊙	210	Lavender
897	◉	221	Shell pink
1006	♥	304	Christmas red
218	▲	319	Dark pistachio
215	☆	320	True pistachio
038	◻	335	Medium rose
214	⊞	368	Light pistachio
1043	⊓	369	Pale pistachio
310	⊕	434	Medium chestnut
098	✳	553	Medium violet
889	◆	610	Drab brown
256	⊟	704	Chartreuse
295	◇	726	Light topaz
1012	:	754	Peach
882	▽	758	Terra-cotta
307	⊠	783	Christmas gold
144	S	800	Delft blue
161	◩	813	Powder blue
160	⊞	826	Bright blue
052	⋀	899	Light rose
1034	✕	931	Antique blue
244	◉	987	Forest green
036	∼	3326	Pale rose
1020	⊟	3713	Salmon
120	⊓	3747	Periwinkle
306	▷	3820	Straw
1048	★	3826	Golden brown

ANCHOR		DMC	
BACKSTITCH			
002	╱	000	White
979	╱	312	Navy
218	╱	319	Dark pistachio
038	╱	335	Medium rose
401	╱	413	Pewter
358	╱	433	Dark chestnut
102	╱	550	Deep violet
309	╱	781	Dark topaz
043	╱	815	Garnet
381	╱	938	Coffee brown
244	╱	987	Forest green
STRAIGHT STITCH			
108	╱	210	Lavender
295	╱	726	Light topaz
160	╱	826	Bright blue
052	╱	899	Light rose
036	╱	3326	Pale rose
SATIN STITCH			
038	╱	335	Medium rose
FRENCH KNOT			
002	○	000	White
038	●	335	Medium rose (2X)
401	●	413	Pewter
381	●	938	Coffee brown
306	○	3820	Straw
LAZY DAISY			
244	✎	987	Forest green

valentines

The joyous Christmas season is the perfect time to welcome guests to your home or send a token of love or friendship. In this wonderful assortment of festive designs, you'll find just the right one to stitch for your home or give as a gift. Choose from radiant angels or humble nativity scenes, chiming bells or elegant greetings to share your stitching talents and spread the giving spirit of this miraculous season.

christmas fun

stockings & sweets

inspirations

Merry and bright, these fun Christmas designs are inspired by some of the season's treats and treasures.

ideas

- Make a table runner by alternating the gingerbread boy and girl designs.
- Add a special touch to Christmas dinner by stitching place cards using one of the mini designs (see the alphabets on *pages 242–279* to personalize your place cards).
- Stitch the small candy cane design on perforated plastic to make fun holiday napkin rings.

plate no. 19
stockings and sweets

stockings & sweets

instruction

We stitched the Stockings and Sweets cross-stitch plate, *opposite*, over two threads on 28-count Mint Green (#621) Jubilee fabric. All cross-stitches are completed using two plies of cotton embroidery floss. All other stitches are completed using one ply of floss.

STOCKINGS AND SWEETS

ANCHOR		DMC
002	·	000 White
108		210 Lavender
1006	◆	304 Medium Christmas red
042	◎	309 Rose
9046	✳	321 True Christmas red
977	◇	334 Dark baby blue
150	●	336 Navy
398	∿	415 Pearl gray
310	#	434 Chestnut
1045	▢	436 Tan
212	◆	561 Dark seafoam
210	✕	562 Medium seafoam
206	−	564 Light seafoam
900	◣	648 Beaver gray
226	◩	702 Christmas green
238	△	703 Chartreuse
295	▽	726 Topaz
890	◪	729 Old gold
1022	◯	760 True salmon
1021	◿	761 Light salmon
128	◰	775 Light baby blue
043	♥	815 Garnet
380	▲	838 Beige brown
246	⋈	986 Forest green
292		3078 Lemon
1024	+	3328 Salmon
306	◎	3820 Straw

ANCHOR		DMC
BACKSTITCH		
002	/	000 White
9046	/	321 True Christmas red
150	/	336 Navy
683	/	500 Blue green
206	/	564 Light seafoam
226	/	702 Christmas green
238	/	703 Chartreuse
295	/	726 Topaz
043	/	815 Garnet
380	/	838 Beige brown
1024	/	3328 Salmon
306	/	3820 Straw
FRENCH KNOT		
002	○	000 White
108	●	210 Lavender
9046	●	321 True Christmas red
238	○	703 Chartreuse
295	○	726 Topaz
043	●	815 Garnet
380	●	838 Beige brown
LAISY DAISY		
238	✐	703 Chartreuse
043	✐	815 Garnet

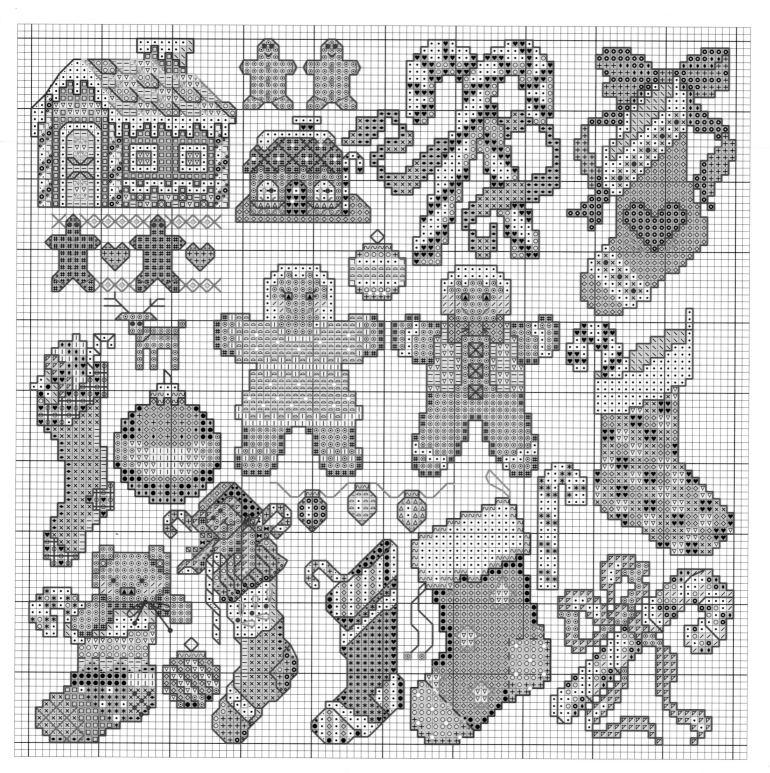

stockings and sweets

sentiments

inspirations
Whether sung, spoken, or written, heartfelt greetings inspire for this uplifting selection of Christmas messages.

ideas

- Use the "Noel" motif to stitch a striking bellpull.
- Make an ornament by stitching the heart and star motif on white cross-stitch fabric and finish in a circular shape, trimming the edge with gold braid.
- Stitch the tiny holly or heart motif on perforated paper to make gift tags.

plate no. 20
sentiments

sentiments

instruction

We stitched the Sentiments cross-stitch plate, *opposite*, over two threads on 28-count Black (#720) Jubilee fabric. All cross-stitches are completed using two plies of cotton embroidery floss or metallic thread. All other stitches are completed using one ply of floss.

SENTIMENTS

ANCHOR		DMC
002	⊡	000 White
1006	⊞	304 Medium Christmas red
9046	▦	321 True Christmas red
011	⊕	350 Medium coral
009	▧	352 Pale coral
923	◆	699 Dark Christmas green
227	⊙	701 True Christmas green
303	▽	742 Tangerine
302	⊟	743 Yellow
132	●	797 Royal blue
131	☒	798 Dark Delft blue
130	◇	809 True Delft blue
013	▲	817 Deep coral
256	△	906 Parrot green
035	⊡	3801 Watermelon
	✳	284Z Gold DMC metallic embroidery thread

ANCHOR		DMC
BACKSTITCH		
1006	╱	304 Medium Christmas red
923	╱	699 Dark Christmas green
308	╱	782 Topaz
045	╱	814 Garnet
	╱	284Z Gold DMC metallic embroidery thread
FRENCH KNOT		
1006	●	304 Medium Christmas red
308	●	782 Topaz

sentiments

holiday greenery

inspirations The greenery of Christmas—garlands and wreaths fashioned from evergreens, holly, and berries—inspire these festive designs.

ideas

- Stitch a sampler of Christmas trees accompanied by the words, "O Christmas Tree" (see the alphabets on *pages 242–279*).
- Embellish premade gold lamé place mats with a simple border of holly and French knot berries.
- Adorn guest towels with a banding of quick-to-stitch poinsettias or holiday garland.

plate no. 21
holiday greenery

holiday greenery

instruction

We stitched the Holiday Greenery cross-stitch plate, *opposite*, over two threads on 28-count Mint Green (#621) Jubilee fabric. All cross-stitches are completed using two plies of cotton embroidery floss. All other stitches are completed using one ply of floss.

HOLIDAY GREENERY

ANCHOR		DMC	
002	⋅	000	White
215	▲	319	Dark pistachio
9046	⊞	321	True Christmas red
1025	▢	347	Salmon
010	◯	351	Coral
1005	✳	498	Dark Christmas red
877	◇	502	Medium blue green
875	╱	503	True blue green
923	◆	699	Dark Christmas green
226	✕	702	Light Christmas green
256	△	704	Chartreuse
295	☆	726	Light topaz
310	◤	780	Deep topaz
132	◆	797	Royal blue
131	⊖	798	Dark Delft blue
130	∼	809	True Delft blue
043	◙	815	Medium garnet
218	⋈	890	Deep pistachio
897	♥	902	Deep garnet
205	⊕	911	Emerald
203	▬	954	Nile green
246	●	986	Dark forest green
244	⊞	987	Medium forest green
242	⊙	989	Pale forest green
266	◿	3347	Medium yellow green
264	▽	3348	Light yellow green
033	♡	3706	Medium watermelon
031	◺	3708	Light watermelon
386	⊡	3823	Yellow
890	▨	3829	Old gold

ANCHOR		DMC	
BACKSTITCH			
002	╱	000	White
9046	╱	321	True Christmas red
923	╱	699	Dark Christmas green
226	╱	702	Light Christmas green
310	╱	780	Deep topaz
043	╱	815	Medium garnet
382	╱	3371	Black-brown
236	╱	3799	Charcoal
890	╱	3829	Old gold
FRENCH KNOT			
1005	●	498	Dark Christmas red
306	●	3820	Straw

holiday greenery

holiday traditions

inspirations

The glowing sights and familiar sounds of the Christmas season inspire these traditional holiday cross-stitch designs.

ideas

- Make Christmas dinner one to remember by trimming the corners of premade linen napkins with stitched jingle bell motifs.
- Stitch a border of holiday lights around the edges of a table mat.
- For a make-it-in-minutes gift tag, stitch a single candle, package, or reindeer on perforated paper.

plate no. 22
holiday traditions

holiday traditions

instruction

We stitched the Holiday Traditions cross-stitch plate, *opposite*, over two threads on 28-count Teal Green (#626) Lugana fabric. All cross-stitches are completed using two plies of cotton embroidery floss. All other stitches are completed using one ply of floss.

HOLIDAY TRADITIONS

ANCHOR		DMC	
002	⋅	000	White
895	∾	223	Shell pink
148	◪	311	True navy
9046	◉	321	Christmas red
978	⊖	322	Pale navy
010	▷	351	Coral
008	╱	353	Peach
878	◆	501	Dark blue green
875	◪	503	True blue green
280	▣	581	True moss green
8581	▢	646	Medium beaver gray
900	◺	648	Light beaver gray
901	◉	680	Old gold
227	✕	701	Christmas green
256	△	704	Chartreuse
305	═	725	True topaz
295	▽	726	Light topaz
310	◆	780	Deep topaz
309	⊕	781	Dark topaz
308	◗	782	Medium topaz
307	✳	783	Christmas gold
144	⬚	800	Pale Delft blue
130	◇	809	True Delft blue
043	♥	815	Medium garnet
380	▲	838	Deep beige brown
379	◨	840	Medium beige brown
035	✚	891	Carnation
897	●	902	Deep garnet
1010	─	951	Ivory
292	▯	3078	Pale lemon
267	⋈	3346	Hunter green
033	◎	3706	Watermelon
273	⊞	3787	Brown gray
278	◿	3819	Light moss green

ANCHOR		DMC	
BACKSTITCH			
148	╱	311	True navy
9046	╱	321	Christmas red
978	╱	322	Pale navy
305	╱	725	True topaz
310	╱	780	Deep topaz
380	╱	838	Deep beige brown
218	╱	890	Pistachio
897	╱	902	Deep garnet
267	╱	3346	Hunter green
382	╱	3371	Black brown
273	╱	3787	Brown gray
STRAIGHT STITCH			
002	╱	000	White
295	╱	726	Light topaz
STAR STITCH			
227	✳	701	Christmas green
FRENCH KNOT			
002	○	000	White
9046	●	321	Christmas red
295	◒	726	Light topaz
380	●	838	Deep beige brown
382	●	3371	Black-brown
FEATHER STITCH			
875	╱	503	True blue green
267	╱	3346	Hunter green
LAZY DAISY			
010	⬭	351	Coral
280	⬭	581	True moss green
267	⬭	3346	Hunter green

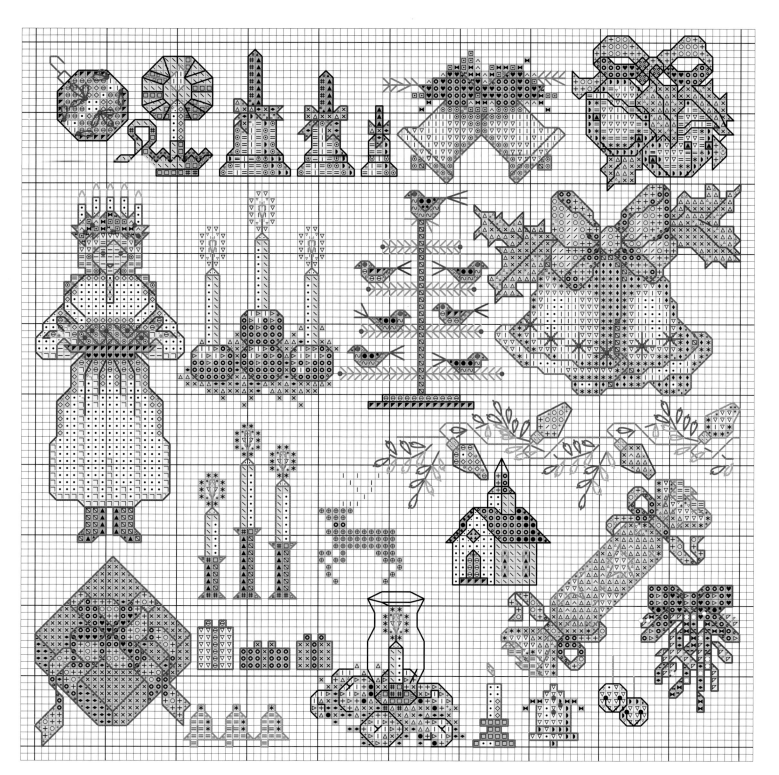

holiday traditions

angels &
nativity scenes

Scenes of
the first Christmas and
joyful angels inspire
this glorious treasury
of holiday designs.

ideas

- Stitch cherubs on pale-colored fabrics to make ornaments that will be cherished for generations.
- Turn a small stitched angel into a brooch for a special angel in your life.
- Stitch one of the larger angels on perforated plastic and attach it to a pillar candle using straight pins.

plate no. 23
angels and nativity scenes

angels & nativity scenes

instruction

We stitched the Angels and Nativity Scenes cross-stitch plate, *opposite*, over two threads on 28-count Misty Blue (#594) Cashel Linen fabric. All cross-stitches are completed using two plies of cotton embroidery floss. All other stitches are completed using one ply of floss.

ANGELS AND NATIVITY SCENES

ANCHOR		DMC	
002	⊡	000	White
110	◈	208	Dark lavender
109	⊙	209	Medium lavender
342	⁄	211	Pale lavender
1049	⊠	301	Medium mahogany
403	■	310	Black
013	◉	349	Dark coral
011	⊞	350	Medium coral
358	●	433	Chestnut
1045	□	436	Tan
212	◆	561	Seafoam
900	⊟	648	Beaver gray
886	⟍	677	Old gold
226	⊠	702	Christmas green
238	△	703	Chartreuse
295	☆	726	Topaz
1021	♡	761	Salmon
161	⊖	826	Bright blue
380	▲	838	Beige brown
205	◉	911	Emerald
881	⊟	945	Ivory
292	⊡	3078	Lemon
144	◇	3325	Baby blue
1008	∿	3773	Rose beige
1015	♥	3777	Terra-cotta
306	✳	3820	Dark straw
874	▽	3822	Light straw

ANCHOR		DMC	
BACKSTITCH			
002	╱	000	White
013	╱	349	Dark coral
161	╱	826	Bright blue
380	╱	838	Beige brown
205	╱	911	Emerald
382	╱	3371	Black brown
306	╱	3820	Dark straw
FRENCH KNOT			
002	○	000	White
013	●	349	Dark coral
205	●	911	Emerald
382	●	3371	Black brown
306	●	3820	Dark straw
DIAMOND EYELET			
002	✳	000	White
306	✳	3820	Dark straw

angels and nativity scenes

the twelve days
of christmas

inspirations Inspired by the popular Christmas carol, stitch these designs separately or frame them as one to enjoy each holiday season.

ideas

- Make a festive square pillow by stitching this design and trimming the edges in holiday plaid.
- Stitch the detailed designs and borders on a strip of fabric horizontally, frame, and hang over a doorway.
- Create a collection of ornaments by stitching the designs individually, then treat with fabric stiffener before hanging.

plate no. 24
the twelve days of christmas

the twelve days of christmas

instruction

We stitched The Twelve Days of Christmas cross-stitch plate, *opposite,* over two threads on 28-count Wedgewood (#501) Lugana fabric. All cross-stitches are completed using two plies of cotton embroidery floss. Blended needle stitches are completed using one ply of each color floss as listed in the key. All other stitches are completed using one ply of floss.

THE TWELVE DAYS OF CHRISTMAS

ANCHOR		DMC	
002	⊡	000	White
403	■	310	Black
9046	◉	321	True Christmas red
008	♡	353	Peach
398	◹	415	Pearl gray
267	◆	469	Dark avocado
266	◎	470	Medium avocado
1005	♥	498	Dark Christmas red
891	◿	676	Light old gold
901	◆	680	Dark old gold
305	▽	725	Topaz
169	⊠	806	Dark peacock blue
168	◇	807	Medium peacock blue
379	⊖	840	Medium beige brown
378	☐	841	True beige brown
035	⊞	891	Carnation
1035	●	930	Dark antique blue
1033	◠	932	True antique blue
881	⊟	945	Ivory
355	▲	975	Deep golden brown
1002	◐	977	Light golden brown
1008	◨	3773	Rose beige
1050	◪	3781	Mocha
306	✳	3820	Straw
1048	⧉	3826	Dark golden brown

ANCHOR		DMC	
BACKSTITCH			
002	╱	000	White
9046	╱	321	True Christmas red
266	╱	470	Medium avocado
380	╱	838	Deep beige brown
355	╱	975	Deep golden brown
306	╱	3820	Straw
BLENDED BACKSTITCH			
212	╱	561	Seafoam (1X) and
876		3816	Celadon green (1X)
STRAIGHT STITCH			
266	╱	470	Medium avocado
881	╱	945	Ivory
FRENCH KNOT			
002	○	000	White
9046	●	321	True Christmas red
305	◐	725	Topaz
380	●	838	Deep beige brown
306	●	3820	Straw
WOVEN RUNNING STITCH			
9046	− −	321	True Christmas red
306	⌃	3820	Straw
LAZY DAISY			
002	⬭	000	White
403	⬭	310	Black
380	⬭	838	Deep beige brown
SMYRNA-CROSS			
1033	✳	932	True antique blue

the twelve days of christmas

F rolicking and jolly, long-awaited winter characters
come to life in this fun-to-stitch chapter destined to
delight children of all ages. While many of these fun
fellows are designed with a whimsical flair, you'll also
enjoy stitching Santas and snowmen that have a
country or traditional twist. With a sprinkling of
snowflake designs to stitch up in a jiffy, our beloved
cold-weather friends will find their way into your
holiday stitching and into your heart.

santas &
snowmen

santas

inspirations Santa Claus, in all shapes and sizes, inspires this group of ever-happy Santas to stitch for a favorite collector or kid at heart.

ideas

- Treat yourself to a pair of holiday earrings by stitching one of the smallest Santa motifs.
- Stitch several designs on perforated plastic, trim, and tie them to a purchased wreath.
- Select a favorite Santa and stitch him on a stocking cuff (to personalize it, see the alphabets on *pages 242–279*).

plate no. 25
santas

santas

instruction

We stitched the Santas cross-stitch plate, *opposite,* over two threads on 28-count Cameo Rose (#484) Cashel Linen fabric. All cross-stitches are completed using two plies of cotton embroidery floss. All other stitches are completed using one ply of floss.

SANTAS

ANCHOR		DMC
002	⊡	000 White
897	◉	221 Shell pink
9046	▢	321 True Christmas red
1025	✚	347 Salmon
011	▷	350 Medium coral
010	ⵈ	351 Light coral
009	◯	352 Pale coral
398	◇	415 Pearl gray
358	▦	433 Chestnut
1005	◈	498 Dark Christmas red
683	◆	500 Blue green
1040	⏀	647 Beaver gray
226	⊖	702 Christmas green
256	✕	704 Chartreuse
308	◆	782 Topaz
043	✤	815 Medium garnet
164	●	824 Deep bright blue
161	◹	826 Medium bright blue
897	♥	902 Deep garnet
258	◲	904 Deep parrot green
255	△	907 Light parrot green
881	⊟	945 Ivory
397	Ⓢ	3024 Brown gray
382	▲	3371 Black brown
031	♡	3708 Light watermelon
1008	◠	3773 Rose beige
306	☆	3820 Straw
386	Ⅰ	3823 Yellow

ANCHOR		DMC
BACKSTITCH		
002	╱	000 White
400	╱	317 True pewter
9046	╱	321 True Christmas red
308	╱	782 Topaz
897	╱	902 Deep garnet
258	╱	904 Deep parrot green
382	╱	3371 Black brown
STRAIGHT STITCH		
002	╱	000 White
FRENCH KNOT		
9046	●	321 True Christmas red
1005	●	498 Dark Christmas red
382	●	3371 Black brown
035	●	3705 Dark watermelon
LAZY DAISY		
002	⬭	000 White
258	⬭	904 Deep parrot green
STAR STITCH		
308	✳	782 Topaz

santas

jolly st. nicks

inspirations

He sees you while you're stitching—the gift-bearing Santa that delights children on Christmas morning inspires these merry designs.

ideas

- Create an heirloom stocking by stitching St. Nick on the front (see the alphabets on *pages 242–279* to include a name).
- Stitch the Santa angel on small-count fabric to make a delightful tree topper.
- Make a holiday quilt by combining favorite holiday designs from *pages 88–125* on a variety of red, green, and white cross-stitch fabrics.

plate no. 26
jolly st. nicks

jolly st. nicks

instruction

We stitched the Jolly St. Nicks cross-stitch plate, *opposite*, over two threads on 28-count Evening Rose (#440) Annabelle fabric. All cross-stitches are completed using two plies of cotton embroidery floss. All other stitches are completed using one ply of floss.

JOLLY ST. NICKS

ANCHOR		DMC	
002	⬚	000	White
1006	⬚	304	Medium Christmas red
399	⬚	318	Steel
9046	⬚	321	True Christmas red
009	⬚	352	Coral
398	⬚	415	Light pearl gray
1046	⬚	435	Chestnut
273	⬚	645	Dark beaver gray
1040	⬚	647	True beaver gray
900	⬚	648	Light beaver gray
046	⬚	666	Red
923	⬚	699	Dark Christmas green
227	⬚	701	True Christmas green
256	⬚	704	Chartreuse
295	⬚	726	Topaz
882	⬚	758	Light terra-cotta
234	⬚	762	Pale pearl gray
307	⬚	783	Christmas gold
1005	⬚	816	Light garnet
162	⬚	825	Dark bright blue
161	⬚	826	Medium bright blue
897	⬚	902	Deep garnet
274	⬚	928	Gray blue
881	⬚	945	Ivory
1011	⬚	948	Peach
391	⬚	3033	Mocha
382	⬚	3371	Black brown
033	⬚	3706	Medium watermelon
031	⬚	3708	Light watermelon
868	⬚	3779	Pale terra-cotta
278	⬚	3819	Moss green
306	⬚	3820	Straw

ANCHOR		DMC	
BACKSTITCH			
002	╱	000	White
9046	╱	321	True Christmas red
273	╱	645	Dark beaver gray
227	╱	701	True Christmas green
307	╱	783	Christmas gold
382	╱	3371	Black brown
FRENCH KNOT			
002	●	000	White
9046	●	321	True Christmas red
227	●	701	True Christmas green
382	●	3371	Black brown
LAZY DAISY			
002	⟋	000	White
9046	⟋	321	True Christmas red
227	⟋	701	True Christmas green

jolly st. nicks

winter characters

inspirations
Inspired by smiling fellows made of snow (and the jolly ol' elf himself!), these characters, full of glee, will warm your heart on even the coldest of winter days.

ideas

- Use waste canvas to add one of these winter-white snowmen to a plain red winter scarf.
- Work a row of Christmas trees in duplicate-stitch across the yoke area of a knit sweater.
- Stitch several star snowman on plastic canvas and join them together with ribbon to make a holiday garland for the tree, mantel, or banister.

plate no. 27
winter characters

winter characters

instruction

We stitched the Winter Characters cross-stitch plate, *opposite*, over two threads on 28-count Ice Blue (#550) Jubilee fabric. All cross-stitches are completed using two plies of cotton embroidery floss. All other stitches are completed using one ply of floss.

WINTER CHARACTERS

ANCHOR		DMC
002	⬚	000 White
403	■	310 Black
399	▢	318 Steel
9046	⊞	321 Christmas red
977	◇	334 Dark baby blue
226	◉	702 Christmas green
295	▽	726 Topaz
316	⊕	740 Tangerine
128	⊟	775 Light baby blue
131	⊖	798 Delft blue
1005	◙	816 Garnet
229	◆	910 True emerald
209	✕	912 Light emerald
381	▲	938 Coffee brown
881	⌐	945 Ivory
203	△	954 Nile green
144	⧄	3325 True baby blue
036	♡	3326 Rose
035	▷	3705 Dark watermelon
033	⊙	3706 Medium watermelon
1020	⌃	3713 Salmon
869	⟍	3743 Antique violet
306	✳	3820 Straw
386	⎮	3823 Yellow
890	◩	3829 Old gold

ANCHOR		DMC
BACKSTITCH		
002	╱	000 White
403	╱	310 Black
9046	╱	321 Christmas red
683	╱	500 Blue green
226	╱	702 Christmas green
131	╱	798 Delft blue
1005	╱	816 Garnet
381	╱	938 Coffee brown
890	╱	3829 Old gold
FRENCH KNOT		
002	●	000 White
403	●	310 Black
9046	●	321 Christmas red
381	●	938 Coffee brown

winter characters

This priceless assortment of border designs mimmicks many patterns found in the world around us. From the rows of soft and fragrant blossoms we await each spring to intricately constructed moldings on century-old buildings, we've captured a variety of styles and color combinations for you to create using your floss-threaded needle.

borders & patterns

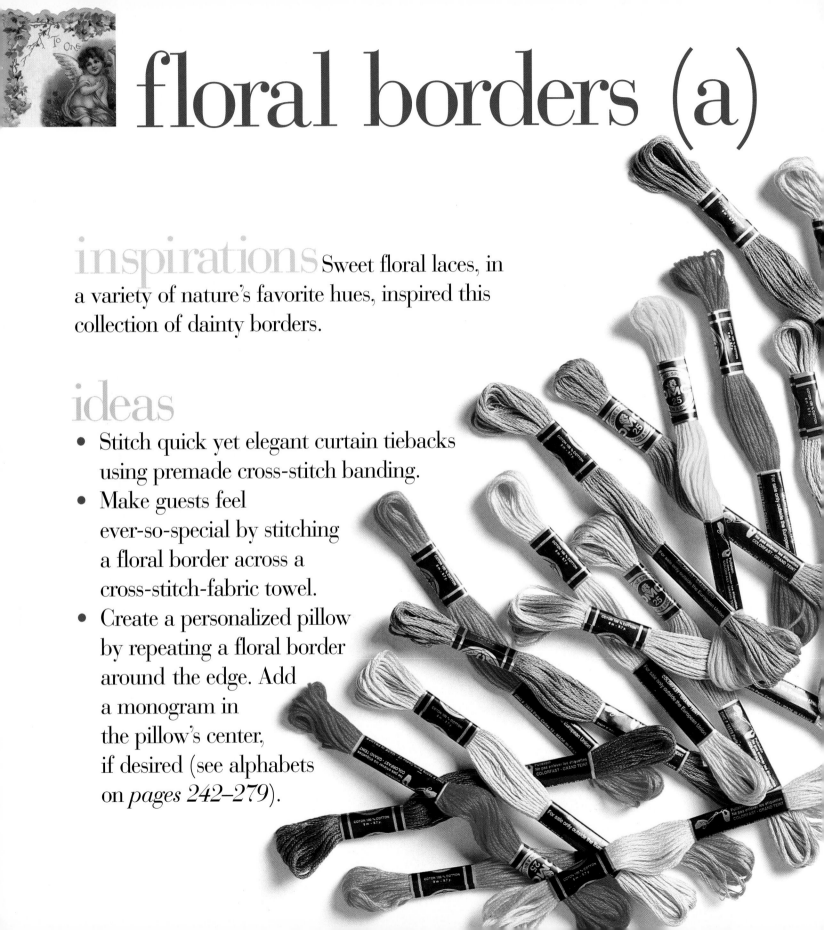

floral borders (a)

inspirations
Sweet floral laces, in a variety of nature's favorite hues, inspired this collection of dainty borders.

ideas

- Stitch quick yet elegant curtain tiebacks using premade cross-stitch banding.
- Make guests feel ever-so-special by stitching a floral border across a cross-stitch-fabric towel.
- Create a personalized pillow by repeating a floral border around the edge. Add a monogram in the pillow's center, if desired (see alphabets on *pages 242–279*).

plate no. 28
floral borders (a)

floral borders (a)

instruction

We stitched the Floral Borders (A) cross-stitch plate, *opposite*, over two threads on 28-count Black (#720) Lugana fabric. All cross-stitches are completed using two plies of cotton embroidery floss. All other stitches are completed using one ply of floss.

FLORAL BORDERS (A)

ANCHOR		DMC
002	⊡	000 White
108	⊟	210 Lavender
042	◉	309 Dark rose
100	◆	327 Antique violet
038	⊕	335 Medium rose
1025	✳	347 Salmon
010	▷	351 Coral
008	⊟	353 Peach
098	⊖	553 Violet
212	◆	561 Dark seafoam
208	▽	563 True seafoam
281	▲	580 Dark moss green
280	◉	581 True moss green
062	⊞	603 True cranberry
055	○	604 Light cranberry
050	∧	605 Pale cranberry
305	▽	725 True topaz
295	▯	726 Light topaz
303	☆	742 Tangerine
177	▼	792 Dark cornflower blue
176	◇	793 Medium cornflower blue
052	♡	899 Light rose
897	♥	902 Garnet
209	⊠	912 Emerald
206	∿	966 Baby green
244	⊞	987 Medium forest green
242	△	989 Pale forest green
264	╱	3348 Yellow green
120	◣	3747 Periwinkle
167	▢	3766 Peacock blue
168	◉	3810 Turquoise

ANCHOR		DMC
BACKSTITCH		
108	╱	210 Lavender
038	╱	335 Medium rose
062	╱	603 True cranberry
177	╱	792 Dark cornflower blue
176	╱	793 Medium cornflower blue
359	╱	801 Coffee brown
209	╱	912 Emerald
268	╱	937 True pine green
168	╱	3810 Turquoise
FRENCH KNOT		
295	●	726 Light topaz
LAZY DAISY		
209	⟡	912 Emerald
268	⟡	937 True pine green

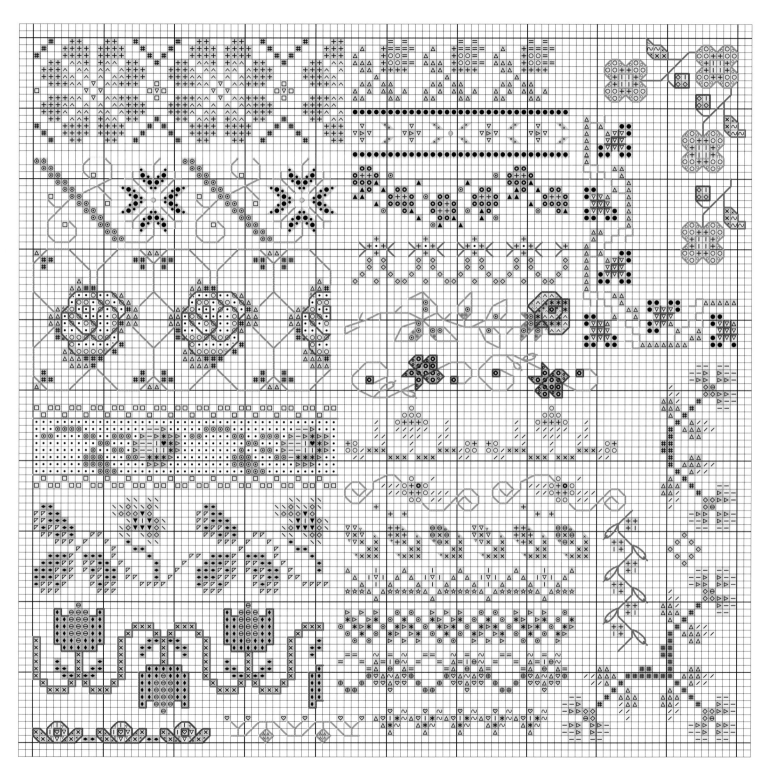

floral borders (a)

floral borders (b)

inspirations

Vivid warm-weather blooms inspired these lovely floral borders that add a touch of summer any time of the year.

ideas

- Add any one of these delicate borders to make fresh-as-a-daisy table linens.
- Create an unforgettable gift bag by stitching one of the quick-as-a-wink borders around the top edge.
- Center and stitch three duplicate motifs across the bib of a little girl's jumper.

plate no. 29
floral borders (b)

floral borders (b)

instruction

We stitched the Floral Borders (B) cross-stitch plate, *opposite*, over two threads on 28-count Black (#720) Lugana fabric. All cross-stitches are completed using two plies of cotton embroidery floss. All other stitches are completed using one ply of floss.

FLORAL BORDERS (B)

ANCHOR		DMC	
002	⋅	000	White
109	⊠	209	Lavender
042	♥	309	Rose
010	○	351	Light coral
009	╱	352	Pale coral
008	⊞	353	Peach
288	▽	445	Lemon
266	▢	470	Medium avocado
253	▤	471	Light avocado
099	◆	552	Violet
256	⊞	704	Chartreuse
295	△	726	Light topaz
309	◉	781	Dark topaz
131	★	798	Dark Delft blue
136	⊙	799	Medium Delft blue
028	♡	893	Carnation
257	✳	905	Parrot green
1003	⊠	922	Copper
269	◈	936	Pine green
381	■	938	Coffee brown
1002	▽	977	Golden brown
246	▲	986	Dark forest green
244	⏀	987	Medium forest green
242	−	989	Pale forest green
144	◲	3325	Baby blue
268	❖	3345	Hunter green
264	▣	3347	Yellow green
087	◉	3607	Dark fuchsia
085	‖	3609	Light fuchsia
5975	⊕	3830	True terra-cotta

ANCHOR		DMC	
BACKSTITCH			
002	╱	000	White
398	╱	415	Pearl gray
267	╱	469	Dark avocado
266	╱	470	Medium avocado
1003	╱	922	Copper
381	╱	938	Coffee brown
268	╱	3345	Hunter green
1015	╱	3777	Deep terra-cotta
FRENCH KNOT			
295	○	726	Light topaz
1003	○	922	Copper
381	●	938	Coffee brown
268	●	3345	Hunter green
LAZY DAISY			
267	✿	469	Dark avocado
144	✿	3325	Baby blue

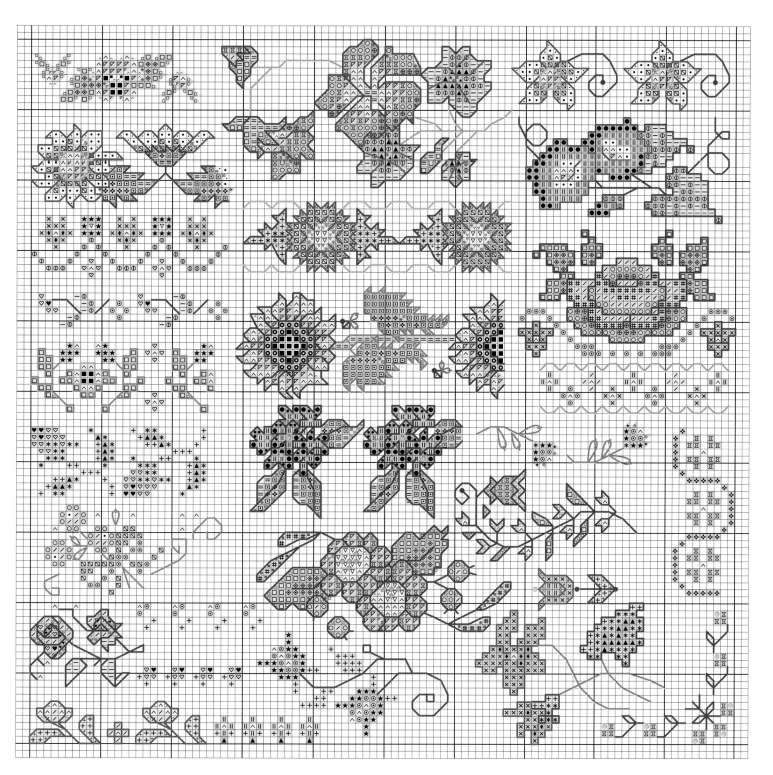

floral borders (b)

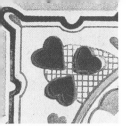

heart borders

inspirations Lacy or country-style, geometric or floral—hearts of all colors and kinds inspired these borders, which will bring joy to your heart and home.

ideas

- Brighten a baby's bib with a horizontal row of hearts.
- Make a quick gift card by stitching one heart on perforated paper.
- Stitch a simple border design on perforated paper or plastic canvas to make a picture frame.

plate no. 30
heart borders

heart borders

instruction

We stitched the Heart Borders cross-stitch plate, *opposite*, over two threads on 28-count New Khaki (#307) Lugana fabric. All cross-stitches are completed using two plies of cotton embroidery floss. All other stitches are completed using one ply of floss.

HEART BORDERS

ANCHOR		DMC	
002	⊡	000	White
110	◆	208	Dark lavender
109	☒	209	Medium lavender
1006	♥	304	Christmas red
978	⊞	322	Navy
011	⊙	350	Coral
217	☆	367	Pistachio
055	▽	604	Cranberry
238	⊟	703	Chartreuse
295	∧	726	Topaz
130	○	809	Delft blue
028	♡	893	Carnation
1044	▲	895	Hunter green
204	⊕	913	Medium Nile green
206	⊞	955	Pale Nile green
076	◉	961	Dark rose pink
075	☐	962	Medium rose pink
298	★	972	Canary
244	⊠	987	Medium forest green
243	�captureL	988	Light forest green
328	◇	3341	Melon
025	⠢	3716	Light rose pink
177	⊕	3807	Cornflower blue

ANCHOR		DMC	
BACKSTITCH			
109	╱	209	Medium lavender
978	╱	322	Navy
217	╱	367	Pistachio
401	╱	413	Pewter
130	╱	809	Delft blue
076	╱	961	Dark rose pink
243	╱	988	Light forest green
059	╱	3350	Dusty rose

heart borders

geometric borders

inspirations Repetitive geometric shapes—found in architecture, on ribbons, in patterns on rugs and tile—inspired this colorful collection that intrigues and delights the eye.

ideas

- Use waste canvas to stitch these pretty patterns on the edges of pillowcases and flat sheets.
- Make an apron from gingham and create a beautiful hem by stitching one of these borders in the squares around the bottom edge of the skirt.
- Stitch several of these borders in rows on a square or rectangular piece of fabric to create a one-of-a-kind pillow for a den or study.

plate no. 31
geometric borders

geometric borders

instruction

We stitched the Geometric Borders cross-stitch plate, *opposite*, over two threads on 28-count New Khaki (#307) Lugana fabric. All cross-stitches are completed using two plies of cotton embroidery floss. All other stitches are completed using one ply of floss.

GEOMETRIC BORDERS

ANCHOR		DMC	
002	⊡	000	White
1049	⊞	301	Mahogany
148	●	311	True navy
218	◆	319	Pistachio
978	☒	322	Pale navy
119	◆	333	Deep periwinkle
977	◇	334	Baby blue
118	◪	340	Medium periwinkle
117	Ⅰ	341	Light periwinkle
009	⊟	352	Coral
210	◸	562	Medium seafoam
208	◹	563	True seafoam
168	◠	597	Turquoise
936	◩	632	Cocoa
045	♥	814	Garnet
244	◉	987	Medium forest green
243	△	988	Light forest green
1024	◎	3328	Salmon
068	⊞	3687	True mauve
170	▲	3765	Peacock blue
069	◙	3803	Dark mauve
177	⊖	3807	Cornflower blue
306	✳	3820	Dark straw
874	▽	3822	Light straw
363	▢	3827	Golden brown
890	★	3829	Old gold

ANCHOR		DMC	
BACKSTITCH			
002	╱	000	White
148	╱	311	True navy
045	╱	814	Garnet
244	╱	987	Medium forest green
177	╱	3807	Cornflower blue
890	╱	3829	Old gold
STAR STITCH			
148	✳	311	True navy
119	✳	333	Deep periwinkle
068	✳	3687	True mauve
874	✳	3822	Light straw

geometric borders

personalized patterns (a)

inspirations Favorite finds in nature plus delicate bows and scrolls are the inspiration for this group of carefully planned designs that beckons to be personalized for someone close to your heart. Use some of the alphabets on *pages 242–279* to complete these designs.

ideas

- Personalize a book or Bible cover using one of these designs and evenweave fabric.
- Stitch personalized luggage tags on perforated plastic to help you identify your bags at a glance.
- Spruce up a blouse by stitching the tulip design and your first initial onto the pocket using waste canvas.

plate no. 32
personalized patterns (a)

personalized patterns (a)

instruction

We stitched the Personalized Patterns (A) cross-stitch plate, *opposite*, over two threads on 28-count Wedgewood (#501) Lugana fabric. All cross-stitches are completed using two plies of cotton embroidery floss. All other stitches are completed using one ply of floss.

PERSONALIZED PATTERNS (A)

ANCHOR		DMC
002	·	000 White
108	∕	210 Lavender
100	◆	327 Antique violet
117	◣	341 Periwinkle
009	▷	352 Coral
217	◪	367 Pistachio
310	⊞	434 Chestnut
683	●	500 Blue green
167	∼	598 Medium turquoise
392	▢	642 Medium beige gray
307	✳	783 Topaz
177	✕	792 Dark cornflower blue
176	◇	793 Medium cornflower blue
023	−	818 Pink
390	⏽	822 Pale beige gray
1044	◆	895 Hunter green
257	◉	905 Parrot green
850	⊖	926 Gray blue
244	⊟	987 Medium forest green
242	△	989 Pale forest green
905	▲	3021 Brown gray
068	◙	3687 True mauve
060	⊞	3688 Medium mauve
069	♥	3803 Dark mauve
305	▽	3821 Straw
9575	◎	3824 Melon

ANCHOR		DMC
BACKSTITCH		
100	∕	327 Antique violet
168	∕	597 Light turquoise
177	∕	792 Dark cornflower blue
1044	∕	895 Hunter green
382	∕	3371 Black brown
236	∕	3799 Charcoal
069	∕	3803 Dark mauve
FRENCH KNOT		
382	●	3371 Black brown

personalized patterns (a)

personalized patterns (b)

inspirations Childhood pleasures and fanciful flowers are the inspiration for these lovable designs that can be personalized using alphabets from *pages 242–279*.

ideas

- Make a name plaque for a child's room by stitching the jump rope or kite motif on small-count fabric.

- Show the cook in the family your appreciation by stitching the "Kiss the Cook" design on a hot pad or apron.

- Personalize a dresser scarf by encircling the first letter of your last name with the rose motif.

plate no. 33
personalized patterns (b)

personalized patterns (b)

instruction

We stitched the Personalized Patterns (B) cross-stitch plate, *opposite,* over two threads on 28-count Cameo Rose (#484) Cashel Linen fabric. All cross-stitches are completed using two plies of cotton embroidery floss. All other stitches are completed using one ply of floss.

PERSONALIZED PATTERNS (B)

ANCHOR		DMC
002	⊡	000 White
403	■	310 Black
100	◆	327 Antique violet
1025	◉	347 Deep salmon
358	▲	433 Dark chestnut
1046	◎	435 Light chestnut
290	☆	444 Lemon
267	◗	469 Avocado
098	◓	553 Violet
280	≡	581 Moss green
055	○	604 Light cranberry
050	♡	605 Pale cranberry
898	⊞	611 Dark drab brown
832	▢	612 Medium drab brown
295	╱	726 Topaz
303	⊕	742 Tangerine
302	▽	743 True yellow
300	⊪	745 Light yellow
1021	▷	761 Light salmon
131	●	798 Dark Delft blue
136	◇	799 Medium Delft blue
209	▨	912 Emerald
203	∼	954 Nile green
316	◖	971 Pumpkin
1002	⊕	977 Golden brown
433	✕	996 Electric blue
397	◺	3024 Brown gray
1023	＋	3712 Medium salmon
896	♥	3721 Shell pink
778	─	3774 Rose beige
306	✳	3820 Straw

ANCHOR		DMC
BACKSTITCH		
1025	╱	347 Deep salmon
050	╱	605 Pale cranberry
131	╱	798 Dark Delft blue
136	╱	799 Medium Delft blue
360	╱	3031 Mocha
1023	╱	3712 Medium salmon
896	╱	3721 Shell pink
306	╱	3820 Straw
FRENCH KNOT		
403	●	310 Black
100	●	327 Antique violet
1025	●	347 Deep salmon
131	●	798 Medium Delft blue
360	●	3031 Mocha
896	●	3721 Shell pink

two-thousand-one 150 *cross stitch designs*

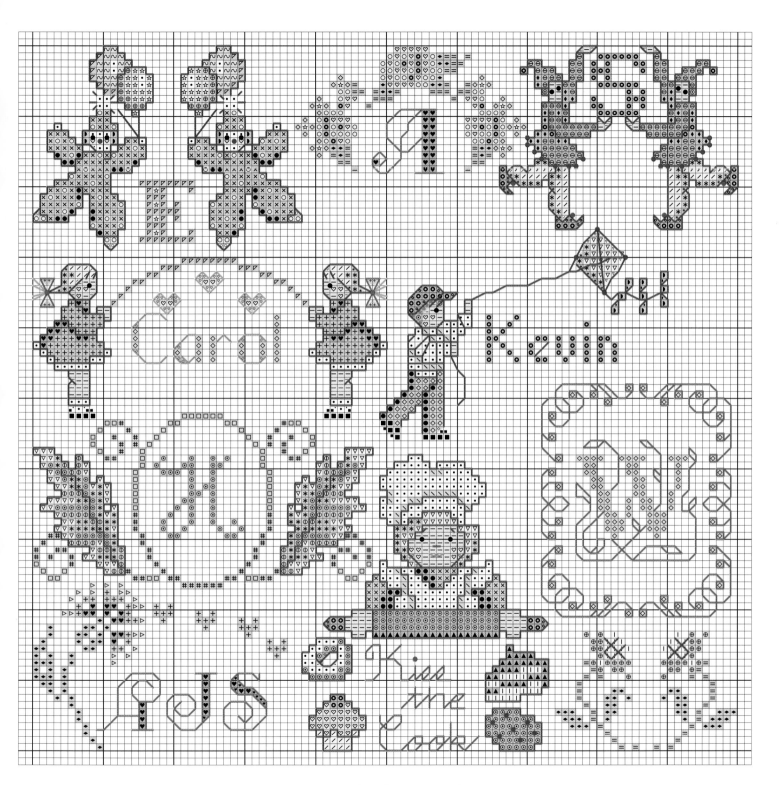

personalized patterns (b)

christmas borders

inspirations
Fun holiday motifs that bring out the child in us all are the inspiration for this merry bunch, which will dance and prance into your holiday stitching.

ideas

- Choose a motif to trim the front of a little one's sweater, remembering that duplicate stitch will make the design slightly shorter and wider.
- Create a unique serving tray by stitching a festive border on fabric and mounting it under the tray's glass.
- Mix and match the border designs to create a very merry tablecloth or table runner edging.

plate no. 34
christmas borders

christmas borders

instruction

We stitched the Christmas Borders cross-stitch plate, *opposite,* over two threads on 28-count Tobacco (#308) Cashel Linen fabric. All cross-stitches are completed using two plies of cotton embroidery floss. All other stitches are completed using one ply of floss.

CHRISTMAS BORDERS

ANCHOR		DMC
002	⋅	000 White
1049	#	301 Mahogany
403	■	310 Black
9046	⊙	321 Christmas red
013	+	349 Coral
398	▫	415 Pearl gray
290	▽	444 Lemon
212	◆	561 Dark seafoam
210	◹	562 Medium seafoam
208	◺	563 True seafoam
228	✕	700 Medium Christmas green
226	△	702 Light Christmas green
295	∧	726 Topaz
302	⁄	743 Yellow
275	∣	746 Off-white
131	◤	798 Dark Delft blue
136	⊖	799 Medium Delft blue
144	◇	800 Pale Delft blue
043	♥	815 Garnet
257	◉	905 Parrot green
881	−	945 Ivory
298	⊕	972 Canary
036	▢	3326 Rose
033	▷	3706 Medium watermelon
035	◈	3801 Deep watermelon
306	✳	3820 Straw

ANCHOR		DMC
BACKSTITCH		
002	╱	000 White
403	╱	310 Black
9046	╱	321 Christmas red
212	╱	561 Dark seafoam
226	╱	702 Light Christmas green
136	╱	799 Medium Delft blue
360	╱	898 Coffee brown
STRAIGHT STITCH		
314	╱	741 Tangerine
FRENCH KNOT		
403	●	310 Black
9046	●	321 Christmas red
360	●	898 Coffee brown

christmas borders

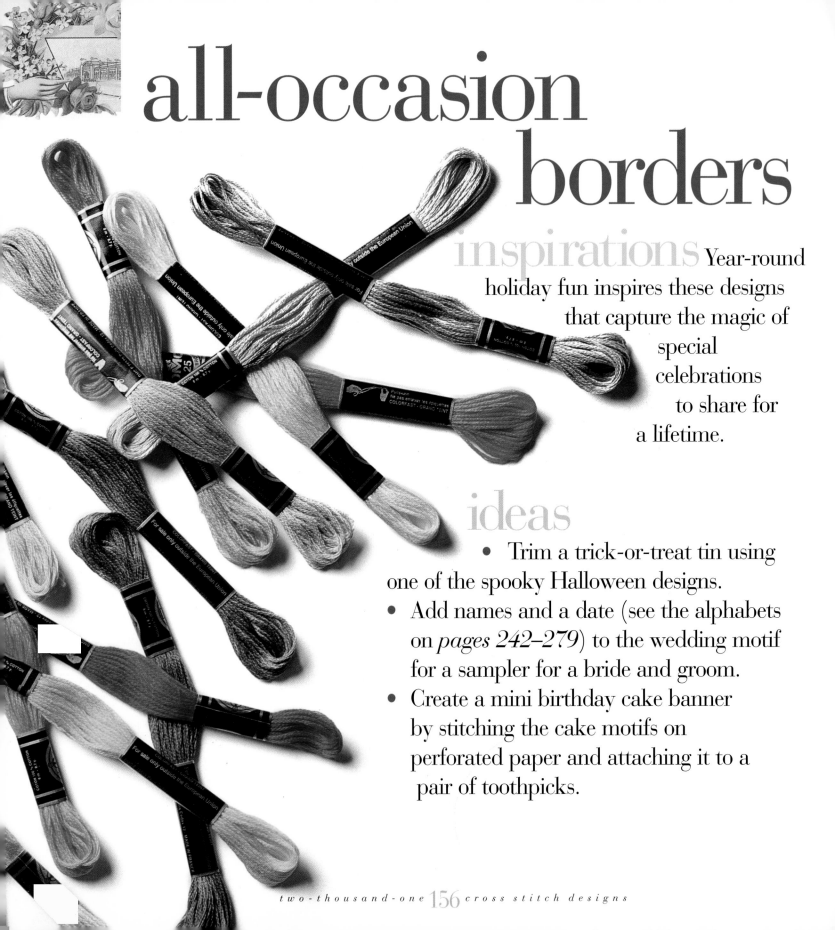

all-occasion borders

inspirations Year-round holiday fun inspires these designs that capture the magic of special celebrations to share for a lifetime.

ideas

- Trim a trick-or-treat tin using one of the spooky Halloween designs.
- Add names and a date (see the alphabets on *pages 242–279*) to the wedding motif for a sampler for a bride and groom.
- Create a mini birthday cake banner by stitching the cake motifs on perforated paper and attaching it to a pair of toothpicks.

plate no. 35
all-occasion borders

all-occasion borders

instruction

We stitched the All-Occasion Borders cross-stitch plate, *opposite*, over two threads on 28-count Carnation Pink (#400) Jubilee fabric. All cross-stitches are completed using two plies of cotton embroidery floss. All other stitches are completed using one ply of floss.

ALL-OCCASION BORDERS

ANCHOR		DMC
002	·	000 White
108	◎	210 Lavender
403	■	310 Black
400	⊠	317 Pewter
013	♥	349 Coral
310	☆	434 Chestnut
099	◆	552 Violet
212	◉	561 Seafoam
293	╱	727 Topaz
314	▢	741 Tangerine
359	⊕	801 Coffee brown
161	⊠	826 Bright blue
205	◈	911 Emerald
881	−	945 Ivory
203	+	954 Nile green
075	◨	962 Medium rose pink
073	⋮	963 Pale rose pink
316	‖	971 Pumpkin
297	∧	973 Canary
059	✦	3350 Dusty rose
140	▽	3755 Baby blue
306	⊞	3820 Dark straw
874	⌐	3822 Light straw
328	S	3825 Bittersweet

ANCHOR		DMC
BACKSTITCH		
403	╱	310 Black
100	╱	327 Antique violet
013	╱	349 Coral
235	╱	414 Steel
310	╱	434 Chestnut
212	╱	561 Seafoam
314	╱	741 Tangerine
161	╱	826 Bright blue
205	╱	911 Emerald
059	╱	3350 Dusty rose
FRENCH KNOT		
403	●	310 Black
235	●	414 Steel
310	●	434 Chestnut
205	●	911 Emerald
075	●	962 Medium rose pink

all-occasion borders

nature & country borders

inspirations

You'll be hard-pressed to pick which motif to stitch first from this fun collection of borders inspired by delightful designs from nature and country living.

ideas

- Add a row of felines across a kitchen towel for a kitty lover.
- Add carrot banding to a terra-cotta pot, and you have a special container for holding small gardening tools.
- Stitch a swarm of bees around the edge of a picnic basket liner.

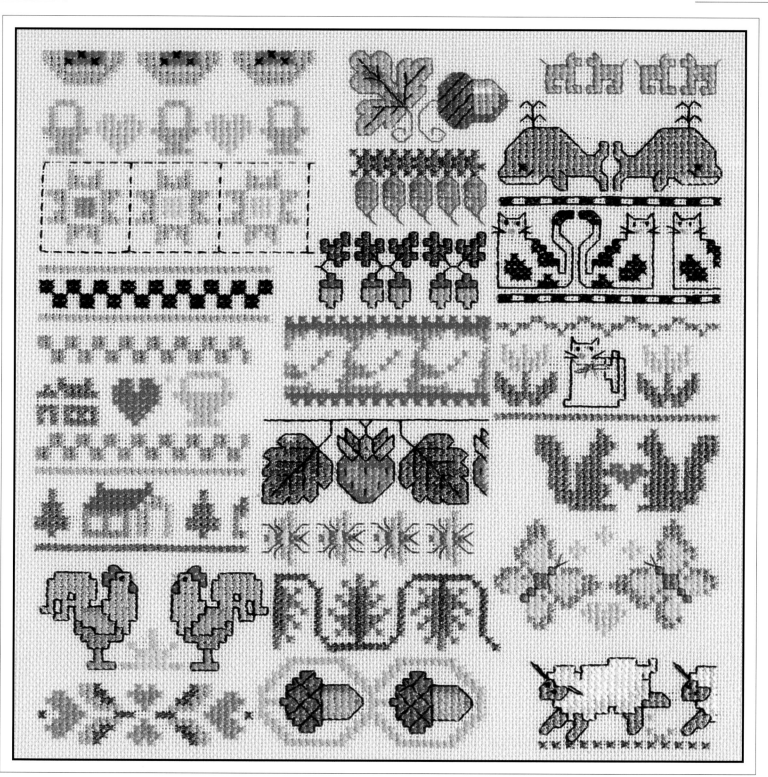

plate no. 36
nature and country borders

nature & country borders

instruction

We stitched the Nature and Country Borders cross-stitch plate, *opposite*, over two threads on 28-count Bone (#253) Lugana fabric. All cross-stitches are completed using two plies of cotton embroidery floss. All other stitches are completed using one ply of floss.

NATURE AND COUNTRY BORDERS

ANCHOR		DMC
002	⊡	000 White
109	◩	209 Lavender
403	◼	310 Black
013	◉	349 Dark coral
010	⊞	351 Light coral
217	⊟	367 Pistachio
351	▲	400 Mahogany
235	◩	414 Steel
310	⊞	434 Chestnut
1045	▢	436 Tan
055	○	604 Cranberry
256	△	704 Chartreuse
324	⊕	721 Bittersweet
295	▽	726 Topaz
176	☒	793 Medium cornflower blue
175	◈	794 Light cornflower blue
161	⊖	826 Bright blue
257	◉	905 Parrot green
204	▨	913 Nile green
1003	◆	922 Copper
1002	◍	977 Golden brown
847	▱	3072 Beaver gray
268	◆	3345 Hunter green
059	♥	3350 Dusty rose
306	✳	3820 Straw
9575	⊟	3824 Melon

ANCHOR		DMC
BACKSTITCH		
403	╱	310 Black
351	╱	400 Mahogany
324	╱	721 Bittersweet
161	╱	826 Bright blue
380	╱	838 Beige brown
FRENCH KNOT		
403	●	310 Black
055	●	604 Cranberry
161	●	826 Bright blue
LAZY DAISY		
403	⬭	310 Black
161	⬭	826 Bright blue

nature and country borders

There's something about country living that warms our souls and makes us feel at home. Maybe it's the charm of a vintage wooden toy or the welcoming glow of an oil lamp burning brightly in the window. Or perhaps it's the scent of a freshly-baked apple pie cooling on the windowsill that beckons us to sit a spell. Whatever you love most about country, we hope you find it to stitch and treasure forever in this chapter of quaint country designs.

country patterns

house & garden motifs

A stroll through a
country house and a
view from the
window inspired these
charming designs that embrace
the best of country.

ideas

- Use waste canvas to stitch a quaint
  teapot or a sprinkling of the kitchen motifs
  on a premade plain place mat.
- Stitch two of the jam designs on perforated
  plastic, cut them out, and attach cording to
  tie around your next gift of homemade jam.
- Stitch the mailbox motif on perforated
  paper and make a card for a
  faraway friend.

plate no. 37
house and garden motifs

house and garden motifs

instruction

We stitched the House and Garden Motifs cross-stitch plate, *opposite,* over two threads on 28-count Ice Blue (#550) Jubilee fabric. All cross-stitches are completed using two plies of cotton embroidery floss. All other stitches are completed using one ply of floss.

HOUSE AND GARDEN MOTIFS

ANCHOR		DMC	
002	⊡	000	White
148	◉	311	True navy
399	✳	318	Steel
1025	◓	347	Salmon
010	▷	351	Coral
398	▨	415	Pearl gray
310	⌗	434	Medium chestnut
1046	▢	435	Light chestnut
231	−	453	Shell gray
267	⋈	469	Avocado
1005	♥	498	Christmas red
212	◆	561	Dark seafoam
210	▣	562	Medium seafoam
280	◹	581	Moss green
891	○	676	Light old gold
886	╱	677	Pale old gold
256	△	704	Chartreuse
326	◆	720	Bittersweet
890	‖	729	Medium old gold
302	▽	743	True yellow
300	▯	745	Light yellow
307	✳	783	Christmas gold
161	◈	813	Medium powder blue
162	⊠	826	Bright blue
160	∿	827	Light powder blue
360	◤	839	Beige brown
257	◉	905	Parrot green
076	⊞	961	Rose pink
316	⊕	971	Pumpkin
355	▲	975	Golden brown
905	★	3021	Brown gray
059	⊛	3350	Dusty rose
1007	⊖	3772	Cocoa
875	◊	3813	Blue green
876	⊟	3816	Celadon green

ANCHOR		DMC	
BACKSTITCH			
399	╱	318	Steel
150	╱	336	Medium navy
1005	╱	498	Christmas red
302	╱	743	True yellow
309	╱	781	Topaz
861	╱	935	Pine green
905	╱	3021	Brown gray
382	╱	3371	Black brown
STRAIGHT STITCH			
1005	╱	498	Christmas red
326	╱	720	Bittersweet
302	╱	743	True yellow
316	╱	971	Pumpkin
FRENCH KNOT			
403	●	310	Black
1025	●	347	Salmon
1005	●	498	Christmas red
LAZY DAISY			
403	⊘	310	Black
1005	⊘	498	Christmas red

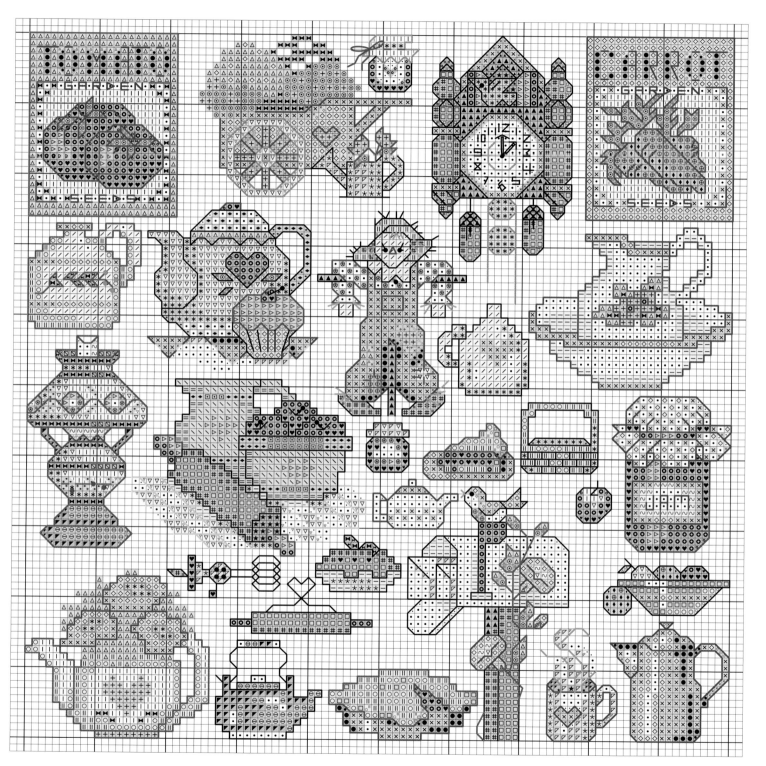

house and garden motifs

country living

inspirations
The comforts of country inspired these heartwarming designs. From a quaint flower-laden cottage to birdhouses big and small, these easy-to-stitch motifs will bring the warmth of country into your home no matter where you live.

ideas

- Create a unique gift for an avid reader by stitching the old-fashioned oil lamp on a premade bookmark.
- Make a great jar topper for your next batch of jelly using one of the apple motifs.
- Stitch the loaf of bread in the corner of a bread cloth, adding "Give Thanks" by using one of the alphabets from *pages 242–279*.

plate no. 38
country living

country living

instruction

We stitched the Country Living cross-stitch plate, *opposite*, over two threads on 28-count New Khaki (#307) Lugana fabric. All cross-stitches are completed using two plies of cotton embroidery floss. Blended backstitch and blended lazy daisy stitches use one ply of each floss color listed. All other stitches are completed using one ply of floss.

COUNTRY LIVING

ANCHOR		DMC	
002	⊡	000	White
9046	☒	321	Christmas red
059	◉	326	Rose
117	⊞	341	Periwinkle
1014	◆	355	Terra-cotta
310	⊡	434	Chestnut
1045	✳	436	Tan
267	▲	469	Avocado
280	◉	581	Moss green
062	☆	603	True cranberry
050	�	605	Pale cranberry
273	⊞	645	Dark beaver gray
1040	⊕	647	True beaver gray
326	◗	720	Bittersweet
295	▽	726	Light topaz
293	ⓢ	727	Pale topaz
279	⧄	734	Olive
1012	⊟	754	Peach
308	⊠	782	Medium topaz
177	●	792	Dark cornflower blue
176	▣	793	Medium cornflower blue
045	♥	814	Garnet
381	■	938	Coffee brown
316	⊞	971	Pumpkin
355	▼	975	Golden brown
397	⦂	3024	Brown gray
268	◩	3345	Hunter green
060	♡	3688	Medium mauve
1031	△	3753	Antique blue
069	★	3803	Dark mauve
306	◆	3820	Dark straw
874	◇	3822	Light straw

ANCHOR		DMC	
BACKSTITCH			
310	╱	434	Chestnut
280	╱	581	Moss green
062	╱	603	True cranberry
295	╱	726	Light topaz
308	╱	782	Medium topaz
178	╱	791	Deep cornflower blue
045	╱	814	Garnet
1041	╱	844	Deep beaver gray
381	╱	938	Coffee brown
397	╱	3024	Brown gray
268	╱	3345	Hunter green
382	╱	3371	Black brown
BLENDED BACKSTITCH			
295	╱	726	Light topaz and
306		3820	Dark straw
FRENCH KNOT			
062	●	603	True cranberry
176	●	793	Medium cornflower blue
381	●	938	Coffee brown
382	●	3371	Black brown
LAZY DAISY			
308	⬭	782	Medium topaz and
295		726	Light topaz
316	⬭	971	Pumpkin

country living

country fun

inspirations

From the barnyard to the backyard, these warmhearted motifs are inspired by sights that reflect the simple country life.

ideas

- Create a country sampler by adding an alphabet (see *pages 242–279*) to the "Bless Our Country Home" design.
- Stitch the goose on perforated paper and add it to the bottom of a glass paperweight.
- Make a quaint-as-country brooch by stitching the rooster on your favorite cross-stitch fabric and finishing it with an oval jewelry mounting piece.

plate no. 39
country fun

country fun

instruction

We stitched the Country Fun cross-stitch plate, *opposite*, over two threads on 28-count New Khaki (#307) Lugana fabric. All cross-stitches are completed using two plies of cotton embroidery floss. All other stitches are completed using one ply of floss.

COUNTRY FUN

ANCHOR		DMC
002	·	000 White
403	■	310 Black
148	●	311 Navy
119	♦	333 Deep periwinkle
118	⊖	340 Medium periwinkle
1025	◎	347 Deep salmon
009	–	352 Coral
1014	◉	355 Dark terra-cotta
5975	▷	356 Medium terra-cotta
267	≡	470 Avocado
936	◉	632 Cocoa
8581	□	646 Medium beaver gray
900	◪	648 Light beaver gray
256	△	704 Chartreuse
890	▽	729 Old gold
308	✳	782 Topaz
176	✕	793 Cornflower blue
359	▦	801 Coffee brown
043	♥	815 Garnet
1024	⊞	3328 Dark salmon
268	◆	3345 Hunter green
382	▲	3371 Black brown
120	◩	3747 Pale periwinkle
169	◩	3760 Wedgewood blue
1048	⊕	3776 Mahogany
874		3822 Straw

ANCHOR		DMC
BACKSTITCH		
002	╱	000 White
119	╱	333 Deep periwinkle
1014	╱	355 Dark terra-cotta
359	╱	801 Coffee brown
382	╱	3371 Black brown
STRAIGHT STITCH		
256	╱	704 Chartreuse
FRENCH KNOT		
002	●	000 White
1025	●	347 Deep salmon
359	●	801 Coffee brown
382	●	3371 Black brown

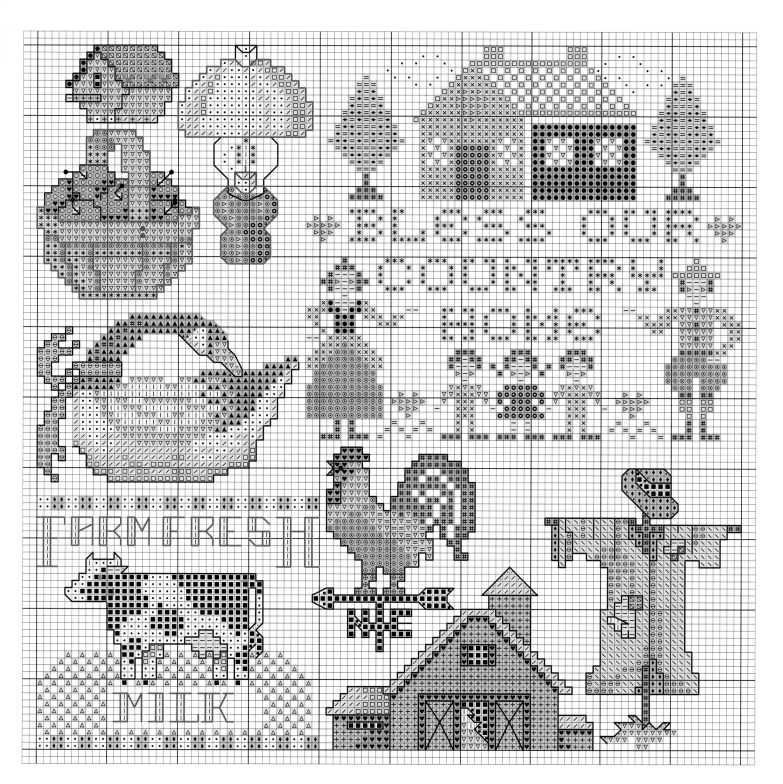

country fun

Renew your pride for America as well as your state, by stitching some of the patriotic- and state-inspired designs in this chapter. Whether you have a passion for Americana or simply want some quick-stitch designs to help celebrate Independence Day, you'll find everything from fragrant state flowers to bold stars and stripes in this memory-making assortment of cross-stitch designs.

americana

patriotic motifs

inspirations Cherished symbols of patriotism and love for the red, white, and blue, inspire this star-spangled collection.

ideas

- Stitch a row of flags to march across a Fourth of July table runner.
- Adorn a pocket with the appropriate year and the USA motif to celebrate the year in style.
- Make a mini banner by stitching several motifs and finishing it with star charms along the bottom edge.

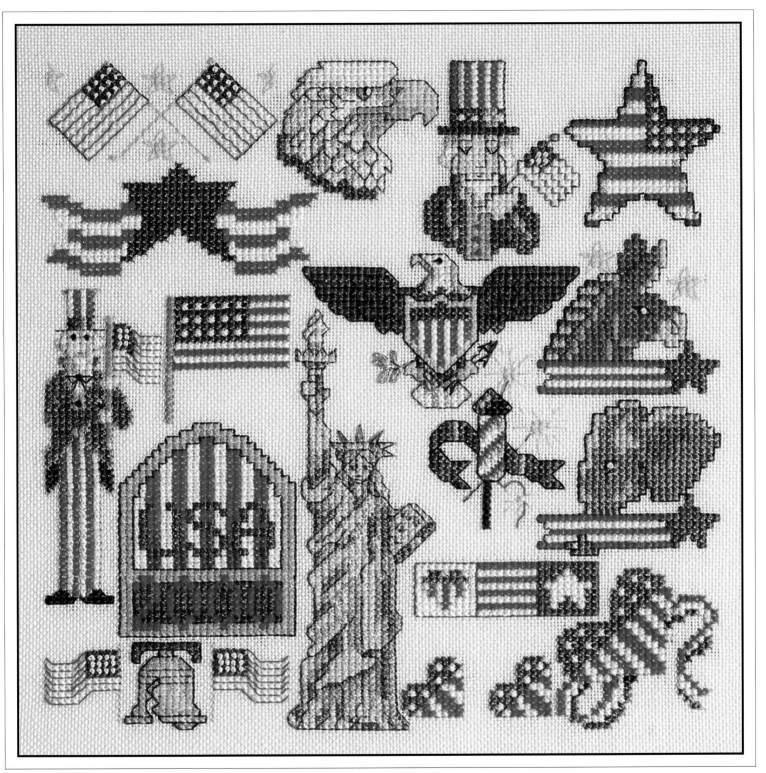

plate no. 40
patriotic motifs

patriotic motifs

instruction

We stitched the Patriotic Motifs cross-stitch plate, *opposite,* over two threads on 28-count Ivory (#225) Jubilee fabric. All cross-stitches are completed using two plies of cotton embroidery floss. All other stitches are completed using one ply of floss.

AMERICANA

ANCHOR		DMC	
002	⊡	000	White
9046	⊞	321	Christmas red
358	◉	433	Dark chestnut
1046	☐	435	Light chestnut
875	△	503	True blue green
1042	⊘	504	Pale blue green
1041	●	535	Ash gray
8581	⊞	646	Medium beaver gray
900	◇	648	Light beaver gray
926			712	Cream
305	▽	725	Topaz
361	▽	738	Tan
1012	♡	754	Peach
307	✳	783	Christmas gold
133	◆	796	Medium royal blue
132	⊖	797	Light royal blue
131	✕	798	Dark Delft blue
130	◸	809	True Delft blue
045	♥	814	Dark garnet
043	◉	815	Medium garnet
1005	◈	816	Light garnet
274	◸	928	Pale gray blue
881	☐	945	Dark ivory
1010	—	951	Medium ivory
905	◩	3021	Brown gray
903	⊟	3032	Mocha
382	▲	3371	Black brown
779	◆	3768	Dark gray blue
306	◎	3820	Dark straw
874	◺	3822	Light straw

ANCHOR		DMC	
BACKSTITCH			
9046	╱	321	Christmas red
305	╱	725	Topaz
307	╱	783	Christmas gold
131	╱	798	Dark Delft blue
043	╱	815	Medium garnet
905	╱	3021	Brown gray
382	╱	3371	Black brown
779	╱	3768	Dark gray blue
STRAIGHT STITCH			
305	╱	725	Topaz
FRENCH KNOT			
002	○	000	White
9046	●	321	Christmas red
305	○	725	Topaz
905	●	3021	Brown gray
382	●	3371	Black brown
LAISY DAISY			
875	⬭	503	True blue green

patriotic motifs

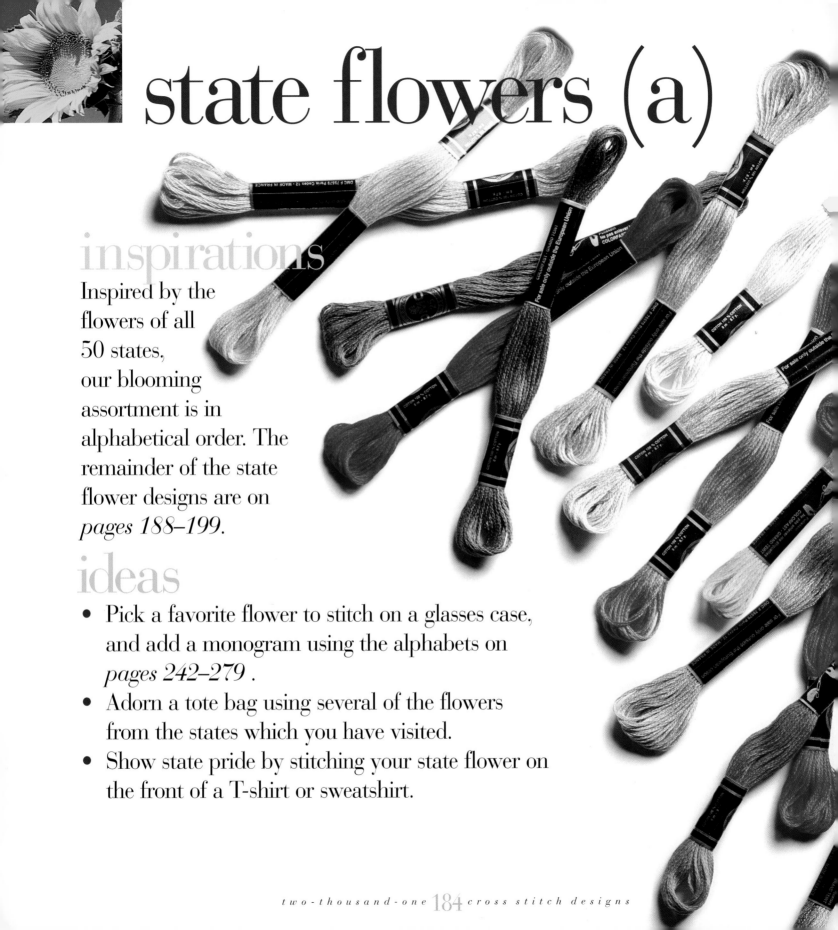

state flowers (a)

inspirations

Inspired by the flowers of all 50 states, our blooming assortment is in alphabetical order. The remainder of the state flower designs are on *pages 188–199.*

ideas

- Pick a favorite flower to stitch on a glasses case, and add a monogram using the alphabets on *pages 242–279 .*
- Adorn a tote bag using several of the flowers from the states which you have visited.
- Show state pride by stitching your state flower on the front of a T-shirt or sweatshirt.

plate no. 41
state flowers (a)

state flowers (a)

instruction

We stitched the State Flowers (A) cross-stitch plate, *opposite*, over two threads on 28-count Mushroom (#309) Lugana fabric. All cross-stitches are completed using two plies of cotton embroidery floss. All other stitches are completed using one ply of floss. The remaining state flower designs are on *pages 188–199.*

STATE FLOWERS (A)

ANCHOR		DMC
002	⊡	000 White
109	⊖	209 Pale lavender
108	⏋	210 Light lavender
218	◆	319 Dark pistachio
215	◸	320 True pistachio
978	⊙	322 Navy
059	✣	326 Deep rose
038	⊛	335 Medium rose
118	◇	340 Medium periwinkle
1025	◗	347 Salmon
310	#	434 Chestnut
233	□	451 Dark shell gray
231	⟍	453 Light shell gray
267	⧄	469 Dark avocado
266	☰	471 Light avocado
253	^	472 Pale avocado
102	♦	550 Deep violet
098	✳	553 Medium violet
256	△	704 Chartreuse
295	▽	726 Light topaz
293	⁄	727 Pale topaz
890	☆	729 Medium old gold
314	★	741 Medium tangerine
303	⊕	742 Light tangerine
275	|	746 Off-white
259	:	772 Loden
131	◩	798 Dark Delft blue
144	∾	800 Pale Delft blue
043	♥	815 Garnet
271	−	819 Pink
257	⊠	905 Parrot green
269	▲	936 Pine green
073	○	963 Rose pink
036	+	3326 Pale rose
268	●	3345 Hunter green
074	♡	3354 Dusty rose
1030	⦶	3746 Dark periwinkle

ANCHOR	DMC
BACKSTITCH	
978 /	322 Navy
309 /	781 Dark topaz
268 /	3345 Hunter green
236 /	3799 Charcoal
STRAIGHT STITCH	
1025 /	347 Salmon
295 /	726 Light topaz
303 /	742 Light tangerine
309 /	781 Dark topaz
268 /	3345 Hunter green
FRENCH KNOT	
978 ●	322 Navy
266 ●	471 Light avocado
295 ●	726 Light topaz
303 ●	742 Light tangerine
236 ●	3799 Charcoal
LAZY DAISY	
236	3799 Charcoal

state flowers (a)

state flowers (b)

inspirations
Blooms found from sea to shining sea inspire these flower motifs—from New Jersey through Kansas.

ideas

- "Grow" any one of these gorgeous blooms on a blouse collar.
- Create a floral "welcome" by stitching a different flower between each of the letters from a chosen alphabet on *pages 242–279*.
- Make a feminine desk accessory set by stitching colorful floral designs on perforated paper and attaching them to a pencil holder, mouse pad, or paperweight.

plate no. 42
state flowers (b)

state flowers (b)

instruction

We stitched the State Flowers (B) cross-stitch plate, *opposite*, over two threads on 28-count Carnation Pink (#400) Jubilee fabric. All cross-stitches are completed using two plies of cotton embroidery floss. All other stitches are completed using one ply of floss. The remaining flower designs are on *pages 184–187* and *pages 192–199*.

STATE FLOWERS (B)

ANCHOR		DMC	
002	·	000	White
109	⊖	209	Pale lavender
108	⌐	210	Light lavender
218	◆	319	Pistachio
978	◉	322	Navy
059	✠	326	Deep rose
038	⊗	335	Medium rose
310	⊞	434	Chestnut
233	□	451	Dark shell gray
231	◤	453	Light shell gray
267	◩	469	Dark avocado
266	≡	471	Light avocado
253	∧	472	Pale avocado
102	◆	550	Deep violet
098	✳	553	Medium violet
891	S	676	Light old gold
256	△	704	Chartreuse
295	▽	726	Light topaz
293	⊘	727	Pale topaz
890	☆	729	Medium old gold
314	✳	741	Medium tangerine
303	⊕	742	Light tangerine
275	Ⅰ	746	Off-white
259	⋮	772	Loden
309	▼	781	Dark topaz
307	‖	783	Christmas gold
136	◿	799	Delft blue
359	◙	801	Coffee brown
043	♥	815	Garnet
271	—	819	Pink
257	✕	905	Parrot green
269	▲	936	Pine green
073	◎	963	Rose pink
036	⊞	3326	Pale rose
268	●	3345	Hunter green
074	♡	3354	Light dusty rose
076	◈	3731	Dark dusty rose

ANCHOR		DMC	
BACKSTITCH			
978	╱	322	Navy
309	╱	781	Dark topaz
268	╱	3345	Hunter green
236	╱	3799	Charcoal
STRAIGHT STITCH			
309	╱	781	Dark topaz
268	╱	3345	Hunter green
FRENCH KNOT			
978	●	322	Navy
891	●	676	Light old gold
295	●	726	Light topaz
293	○	727	Pale topaz
303	●	742	Light tangerine

state flowers (b)

state flowers (c)

inspirations From berries to holly to all kinds of colorful blooms, this handsome grouping is inspired by the flowers from New Mexico to Texas.

ideas

- Use the holly sprig to add a festive touch to purchased fabric holiday napkins.
- Create a keepsake quilt by stitching all of the state flowers on solid fabric using waste canvas.
- Stitch a pretty bloom on the lapel of a woman's cozy bathrobe.

plate no. 43
state flowers (c)

state flowers (c)

instruction

We stitched the State Flowers (C) cross-stitch plate, *opposite*, over two threads on 28-count Wedgewood (#501) Lugana fabric. All cross-stitches are completed using two plies of cotton embroidery floss. All other stitches are completed using one ply of floss. The remaining state flower designs are on *pages 184–191* and *pages 196–199*.

STATE FLOWERS (C)

ANCHOR		DMC
002	⊡	000 White
109	⊖	209 Pale lavender
108	⬓	210 Light lavender
218	◈	319 Dark pistachio
215	◺	320 True pistachio
978	⊙	322 Navy
038	⊛	335 Medium rose
011	◉	350 Coral
310	⊞	434 Chestnut
233	⬜	451 Dark shell gray
267	◻	469 Dark avocado
266	⊟	471 Light avocado
253	⋀	472 Pale avocado
102	◆	550 Deep violet
098	✳	553 Medium violet
891	ⓢ	676 Light old gold
256	△	704 Chartreuse
295	▽	726 Light topaz
293	⊘	727 Pale topaz
890	☆	729 Medium old gold
303	⊕	742 Light tangerine
275	⊡	746 Off-white
259	⋮	772 Loden
309	▼	781 Dark topaz
307	⫼	783 Christmas gold
131	◪	798 Dark Delft blue
136	◿	799 Medium Delft blue
144	∼	800 Pale Delft blue
043	♥	815 Garnet
271	⊟	819 Pink
257	⊠	905 Parrot green
269	▲	936 Pine green
073	◯	963 Rose pink
036	⊞	3326 Pale rose
268	◉	3345 Hunter green
074	♡	3354 Light dusty rose
076	◈	3731 Dark dusty rose

ANCHOR		DMC
BACKSTITCH		
978	╱	322 Navy
236	╱	3799 Charcoal
STRAIGHT STITCH		
1025	╱	347 Salmon
309	╱	781 Dark topaz
FRENCH KNOT		
978	●	322 Navy
295	○	726 Light topaz
293	○	727 Pale topaz
314	●	741 Medium tangerine
359	●	801 Coffee brown
236	●	3799 Charcoal

state flowers (c)

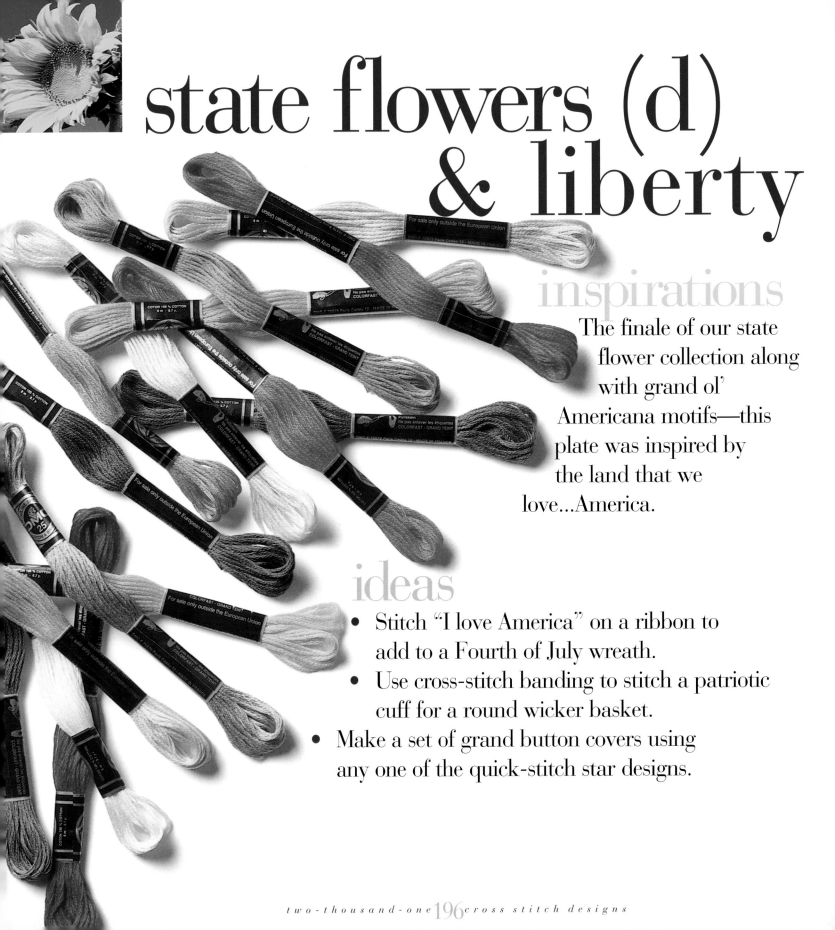

state flowers (d) & liberty

inspirations

The finale of our state flower collection along with grand ol' Americana motifs—this plate was inspired by the land that we love...America.

ideas

- Stitch "I love America" on a ribbon to add to a Fourth of July wreath.
- Use cross-stitch banding to stitch a patriotic cuff for a round wicker basket.
- Make a set of grand button covers using any one of the quick-stitch star designs.

plate no. 44
state flowers (d) and liberty

state flowers (d) & liberty

instruction

We stitched the State Flowers (D) and Liberty cross-stitch plate, *opposite,* over two threads on 28-count Sand (#322) Cashel Linen. All cross-stitches are completed using two plies of cotton embroidery floss. All other stitches are completed using one ply of floss. The remaining state flower designs are on *pages 184–195.*

STATE FLOWERS (D) AND LIBERTY

ANCHOR		DMC
002	⊡	000 White
109	⊖	209 Lavender
218	◆	319 Dark pistachio
215	◪	320 True pistachio
978	◉	322 Navy
059	✣	326 Deep rose
038	⊛	335 Medium rose
011	◖	350 Coral
374	▷	420 Hazel
310	⌗	433 Chestnut
233	▢	451 Shell gray
267	◩	469 Dark avocado
266	⊟	471 Light avocado
253	△	472 Pale avocado
098	✳	553 Violet
256	◭	704 Chartreuse
295	▽	726 Light topaz
293	⧄	727 Pale topaz
259	⠆	772 Loden
144	∼	800 Delft blue
043	♥	815 Garnet
271	⊟	819 Pink
162	◈	825 Bright blue
257	✕	905 Parrot green
269	▲	936 Pine green
269	▯	951 Ivory
073	◎	963 Rose pink
036	✚	3326 Pale rose
268	●	3345 Hunter green
076	◈	3731 Dusty rose
306	◣	3820 Straw
890	★	3829 Old gold

ANCHOR		DMC
BACKSTITCH		
978	╱	322 Navy
358	╱	433 Chestnut
133	╱	796 Royal blue
043	╱	815 Garnet
268	╱	3345 Hunter green
382	╱	3371 Black brown
236	╱	3799 Charcoal
306	╱	3820 Straw
STRAIGHT STITCH		
1025	╱	347 Salmon
309	╱	781 Dark topaz
268	╱	3345 Hunter green
FRENCH KNOT		
978	●	322 Navy
295	●	726 Light topaz
314	●	741 Tangerine
LAZY DAISY		
253	⬭	472 Pale avocado

state flowers (d) and liberty

From one renewing spring to the next, the year is filled with reasons to gather for special times. This chapter is brimming with fun holiday motifs that will add even more joy to your celebrations throughout the year. From parading ducks and bunnies to autumn leaves and prayers of Thanksgiving, you'll find delightful designs to stitch for every joyous season.

year-round holidays

halloween

inspirations
All of the "boo-tiful" motifs that make trick-or-treaters smile (or jump!) are the inspiration for this "spooktacular" cross-stitch collection.

ideas

- Make a band for a treat basket by stitching a ghostly collection of fiends on premade cross-stitch banding.
- Create a sampler by stitching a border of candies around the words "Happy Halloween" (see the alphabets on *pages 242–279*).
- Stitch a jolly jack-o'-lantern with fluorescent floss on a little ghoul's treat bag.

plate no. 45
halloween

halloween

instruction

We stitched the Halloween cross-stitch plate, *opposite,* over two threads on 28-count Lavender (#559) Lugana fabric. All cross-stitches are completed using two plies of cotton embroidery floss. All other stitches are completed using one ply of floss.

HALLOWEEN

ANCHOR		DMC	
002	·	000	White
403	■	310	Black
400	+	317	True pewter
399	○	318	Steel
118	⊠	340	Periwinkle
401	⊞	413	Dark pewter
290	☆	444	Lemon
102	▲	550	Deep violet
099	◉	552	Dark violet
098	◩	553	Medium violet
096	▽	554	Light violet
326	◆	720	Dark bittersweet
323	=	722	Light bittersweet
295	◇	726	Light topaz
293	S	727	Pale topaz
316	✳	740	Dark tangerine
314	◉	741	Medium tangerine
303	∧	742	Light tangerine
310	●	780	Deep topaz
308	▢	782	Medium topaz
256	⊕	906	Medium parrot green
255	▷	907	Light parrot green
881	L	945	Ivory
355	★	975	Golden brown
246	♥	986	Forest green
871	◐	3041	Medium antique violet
144	⊘	3325	Baby blue
382	▼	3371	Black brown
872	◗	3740	Dark antique violet
278	⋮	3819	Moss green

ANCHOR		DMC	
BACKSTITCH			
002	╱	000	White
400	╱	317	True pewter
326	╱	720	Dark bittersweet
303	╱	742	Light tangerine
308	╱	782	Medium topaz
256	╱	906	Medium parrot green
246	╱	986	Forest green
144	╱	3325	Baby blue
382	╱	3371	Black brown
FRENCH KNOT			
002	●	000	White
400	●	317	True pewter
290	○	444	Lemon
326	●	720	Dark bittersweet
382	●	3371	Black brown

halloween

fall & winter holidays

inspirations Special times to celebrate—Thanksgiving, Kwanzaa, and Hanukkah—inspire these glorious designs.

ideas

- Stitch a menorah mantel banner or table runner.
- Create a memorable Thanksgiving table by stitching leaf placecards, pumpkin linen napkins, and a turkey tablecloth.
- Add a cornucopia motif to a bread cloth.

plate no. 46
fall and winter holidays

fall & winter holidays

instruction

We stitched the Fall and Winter Holidays cross-stitch plate, *opposite,* over two threads on 28-count Bone (#253) Lugana fabric. All cross-stitches are completed using two plies of cotton embroidery floss. All other stitches are completed using one ply of floss.

FALL AND WINTER HOLIDAYS

ANCHOR		DMC
002	⊡	000 White
1017	⊠	316 Antique mauve
400	◎	317 Pewter
011	▣	350 Medium coral
009	⊿	352 Pale coral
1014	◆	355 Terra-cotta
854	☆	371 Pecan
351	◉	400 Mahogany
310	◮	434 Chestnut
1045	⊟	436 Dark tan
886	⌊	677 Old gold
226	◇	702 Christmas green
324	⊕	721 Bittersweet
305	⊞	725 True topaz
361	⋀	738 Light tan
301	⊙	744 Yellow
308	⊠	782 Medium topaz
178	▲	791 Cornflower blue
359	◧	801 Coffee brown
013	♥	817 Deep coral
134	◍	820 Royal blue
944	⊞	869 Hazel
340	◪	920 Copper
4146	♡	950 Rose beige
246	★	986 Forest green
410	⌗	995 Electric blue
393	◈	3022 Brown gray
887	‖	3046 Yellow beige
681	▼	3051 Gray green
847	⊟	3072 Beaver gray
266	⊕	3347 Medium yellow green
264	▽	3348 Light yellow green
872	◨	3740 Antique violet
1030	✳	3746 Dark periwinkle
120	⒮	3747 Pale periwinkle
236	◼	3799 Charcoal

ANCHOR		DMC
BACKSTITCH		
351	╱	400 Mahogany
308	╱	782 Medium topaz
178	╱	791 Cornflower blue
359	╱	801 Coffee brown
013	╱	817 Deep coral
340	╱	920 Copper
246	╱	986 Forest green
681	╱	3051 Gray green
236	╱	3799 Charcoal
FRENCH KNOT		
009	◌	352 Pale coral
351	●	400 Mahogany
1045	◌	436 Dark tan
308	◌	782 Medium topaz
681	●	3051 Gray green
236	●	3799 Charcoal
LAZY DAISY		
1045	⬭	436 Dark tan

fall and winter holidays

spring holidays

Inspired by the traditional symbols that help us celebrate those favorite spring holidays, St. Patrick's Day and Easter, these colorful designs can be used in a multitude of ways.

ideas

- Stitch a leprechaun's hat on perforated plastic to make a brooch and a pair of clovers for earrings.
- Use premade banding to create an Easter basket bow using the tiny duck, bunny, and egg designs.
- Make a table mat by stitching a border of large decorated eggs around the edges of a square piece of cross-stitch fabric.

plate no. 47
spring holidays

spring holidays

instruction

We stitched the Spring Holidays cross-stitch plate, *opposite*, over two threads on 28-count Lavender (#559) Lugana fabric. All cross-stitches are completed using two plies of cotton embroidery floss. All other stitches are completed using one ply of floss.

SPRING AND SUMMER HOLIDAYS

ANCHOR		DMC	
002	·	000	White
110	◆	208	Dark lavender
109	⊠	209	Medium lavender
119	◙	333	Periwinkle
977	⊞	334	Dark baby blue
038	⊡	335	Medium rose
010	⊞	351	Light coral
009	╱	352	Pale coral
008	⊟	353	Peach
401	✳	413	Pewter
398	○	415	Pearl gray
374	☆	420	Hazel
253	Ⓢ	472	Avocado
102	▲	550	Deep violet
096	▯	554	Light violet
923	●	699	Dark Christmas green
227	⬚	701	True Christmas green
256	⊟	704	Chartreuse
305	◇	725	True topaz
295	⋀	726	Light topaz
293	∟	727	Pale topaz
890	⊕	729	Old gold
314	▣	741	Tangerine
300	⬂	745	Yellow
275	⠒	746	Off-white
1021	♡	761	Salmon
131	★	798	Dark Delft blue
359	■	801	Medium coffee brown
130	△	809	True Delft blue
160	‖	827	Powder blue
027	∿	894	Carnation
209	▽	912	Emerald
188	◗	943	Aqua
203	✳	954	Nile green
144	⊠	3325	True baby blue
087	♥	3607	Fuchsia

ANCHOR		DMC	
BACKSTITCH			
059	╱	326	Deep rose
401	╱	413	Pewter
209	╱	912	Emerald
340	╱	920	Copper
381	╱	938	Deep coffee brown
FRENCH KNOT			
038	●	335	Medium rose
401	●	413	Pewter
305	○	725	True topaz
027	○	894	Carnation
381	●	938	Deep coffee brown

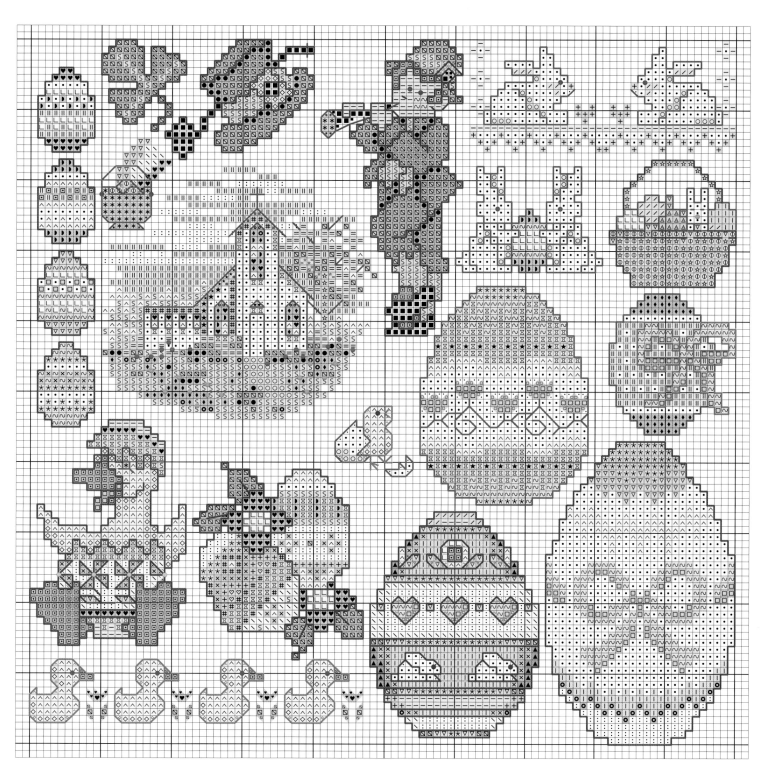

spring holidays

M

other Nature's gifts are reflected in this prized collection to stitch and enjoy. Ever-popular fruit motifs, gentle butterflies, and golden leaves are a few of the cross-stitch designs we're sharing with you in this chapter. Join us for a tour of nature's most beautiful creations which you can recreate using your own stitching talents.

nature designs

fruits & berries

inspirations Some of nature's most delicious treats are the inspiration for these designs rich in color and flavor.

ideas

- Enhance a jar topper using any of these juicy designs.
- Use waste canvas to stitch blueberries on yellow plaid cotton kitchen towels.
- Make a springtime teapot cozy by stitching the rich red cherries randomly on a premade solid cozy.

plate no. 48
fruits and berries

fruits & berries

instruction

We stitched the Fruits and Berries cross-stitch plate, *opposite*, over two threads on 28-count Ice Blue (#550) Lugana fabric. All cross-stitches are completed using two plies of cotton embroidery floss. All other stitches are completed using one ply of floss.

FRUITS AND BERRIES

ANCHOR		DMC	
002	•	000	White
042	⌗	309	Dark rose
148	☆	311	True navy
979	○	312	Light navy
9046	♡	321	Christmas red
038	⊕	335	Medium rose
1025	◎	347	Deep salmon
013	♥	349	Dark coral
010	+	351	Light coral
009	╱	352	Pale coral
362	=	437	Medium tan
334	⊠	606	Orange red
256	∧	704	Chartreuse
305	◇	725	True topaz
293	∟	727	Pale topaz
280	▽	733	Light olive
279	S	734	Pale olive
885	⋮	739	Pale tan
1022	◈	760	True salmon
307	⧄	783	Christmas gold
136	✳	799	Delft blue
359	◆	801	Coffee brown
1005	✤	816	Light garnet
906	●	829	Deep bronze
907	▽	833	Light bronze
257	◗	905	Parrot green
230	⋈	909	Dark emerald
205	◩	911	Medium emerald
1011	⌐	948	Peach
073	∽	963	Rose pink
244	◉	987	Forest green
186	✶	993	Aquamarine
842	◠	3013	Khaki
268	◫	3345	Hunter green
266	☒	3347	Medium yellow green
264	‖	3348	Light yellow green
1015	▼	3777	Terra-cotta
306	⊞	3820	Straw
890	★	3829	Old gold

ANCHOR		DMC	
BACKSTITCH			
002	╱	000	White
150	╱	336	Medium navy
358	╱	433	Chestnut
683	╱	500	Blue green
359	╱	801	Coffee brown
906	╱	829	Deep bronze
897	╱	902	Deep garnet
268	╱	3345	Hunter green
236	╱	3799	Charcoal
FRENCH KNOT			
236	●	3799	Charcoal
LAZY DAISY			
906	⟋	829	Deep bronze

fruits and berries

mother nature (a)

inspirations

Bountiful gardens and the tiny creatures that flutter above them inspired this vibrant collection of plenty.

ideas

- Stitch a family of butterflies on a pillow top.
- Create a fun picnic tablecloth by stitching a few bugs and insects on plaid fabric.
- Stitch an apple in the corner of a cloth napkin to rest under a fruit bowl.

plate no. 49
mother nature (a)

mother nature (a)

We stitched the Mother Nature (A) cross-stitch plate, *opposite,* over two threads on 28-count Bone (#253) Lugana fabric. All cross-stitches are completed using two plies of cotton embroidery floss. All other stitches are completed using one ply of floss.

MOTHER NATURE (A)		
ANCHOR		**DMC**
002	·	000 White
897	▼	221 Shell pink
042	◎	309 Rose
100	⋈	327 Antique violet
1025	◆	347 Deep salmon
013	⊞	349 Dark coral
010	◯	351 Light coral
398	⊞	415 Pearl gray
266	▽	471 Light avocado
253	—	472 Pale avocado
102	⊞	550 Deep violet
098	◉	553 Medium violet
891	△	676 Light old gold
305	☆	725 True topaz
293	⋮	727 Pale topaz
281	✕	732 True olive
279	L	734 Pale olive
275	▯	746 Off-white
1022	⊕	760 True salmon
307	△	783 Christmas gold
1005	♥	816 Garnet
013	★	817 Deep coral
906	●	829 Deep bronze
907	◨	832 Medium bronze
945	S	834 Pale bronze
256	◍	906 Medium parrot green
255	=	907 Light parrot green
850	◲	926 Medium gray blue
848	◪	927 Light gray blue
1011	∧	948 Peach
360	⊠	3031 Mocha
262	⊠	3052 Gray green
1024	✤	3328 Dark salmon
268	◆	3345 Medium hunter green
267	♡	3346 Light hunter green
264	◈	3347 Yellow green
059	✳	3350 Dusty rose
263	▲	3362 Loden
382	■	3371 Black brown
1028	◖	3685 Mauve
1015	⊞	3777 Deep terra-cotta
1013	⫼	3778 True terra-cotta
278	∿	3819 Moss green
890	▶	3829 Deep old gold

ANCHOR		DMC
BACKSTITCH		
279	/	734 Pale olive
360	/	3031 Mocha
382	/	3371 Black brown
STRAIGHT STITCH		
360	/	3031 Mocha
382	/	3371 Black brown
FRENCH KNOT		
360	●	3031 Mocha
382	●	3371 Black brown
LAZY DAISY		
850	∂	926 Medium gray blue
360	∂	3031 Mocha

mother nature (a)

mother nature (b)

From spring pond noises to autumn's rustling leaves, these designs are inspired by the sights and sounds that bring pleasure to our days.

ideas

- Trim a little boy's denim overalls by stitching a frog on the bib and back pocket.
- Use the simple acorn design to make guest placecards that will stitch up in a jiffy.
- Let a bee land on your jacket lapel by stitching it on plastic canvas and attaching a pin back.

plate no. 50
mother nature (b)

mother nature (b)

instruction

We stitched the Mother Nature (B) cross-stitch plate, *opposite,* over two threads on 28-count Mint Green (#621) Jubilee fabric. All cross-stitches are completed using two plies of cotton embroidery floss. All other stitches are completed using one ply of floss.

MOTHER NATURE (B)

ANCHOR		DMC	
403	■	310	Black
1014	▲	355	Dark terra-cotta
5975	✕	356	Medium terra-cotta
310	▢	434	Chestnut
362	☆	437	Tan
253	╱	472	Avocado
281	◉	580	Dark moss green
280	△	581	True moss green
891	⊞	676	Light old gold
256	◯	704	Chartreuse
326	◆	720	Bittersweet
295	⦂	726	Light topaz
293	⌊	727	Pale topaz
316	⌗	740	Dark tangerine
314	⊙	741	Medium tangerine
303	⋀	742	Light tangerine
302	⊠	743	True yellow
301	⊕	744	Medium yellow
307	◹	783	Christmas gold
136	‖	799	Medium Delft blue
130	▽	809	True Delft blue
390	−	822	Beige gray
906	●	829	Deep bronze
277	✳	830	Dark bronze
907	⊖	832	Medium bronze
907	◇	833	Light bronze
945	⑊	834	Pale bronze
360	★	839	Dark beige brown
378	◿	841	True beige brown
257	◈	905	Parrot green
1035	⊞	930	Antique blue
355	▣	975	Golden brown
268	♥	3345	Hunter green
1048	♡	3776	Mahogany
890	✥	3829	Deep old gold

ANCHOR		DMC	
BACKSTITCH			
403	╱	310	Black
1035	╱	930	Antique blue
268	╱	3345	Hunter green
382	╱	3371	Black brown
FRENCH KNOT			
403	●	310	Black
LAZY DAISY			
907	⬭	832	Medium bronze

mother nature (b)

Whether they greet you eagerly at your door or you view them from a distance over a zoo fence, animals of all kinds bring us happiness. In this chapter we've corralled a variety of best-loved animals for you to stitch with your own needle and floss. We hope these fun-to-work designs will strengthen your love for the animal kingdom and bring you a little closer to many of God's creatures, great and small.

animals

wildlife

inspirations

This exotic assortment
is inspired by wild animals from
around the world.

ideas

- Create a one-of-a-kind gift for an animal lover
  by stitching a wildlife favorite and gluing
  it to the back of a hand mirror.
- Use waste canvas to add a colorful parrot to an
  umbrella top.
- Make a tiger paperweight for a handsome
  desk accessory.

plate no. 51
wildlife

wildlife

instruction

We stitched the Wildlife cross-stitch plate, *opposite,* over two threads on 28-count Wedgewood (#501) Lugana fabric. All cross-stitches are completed using two plies of cotton embroidery floss. All other stitches are completed using one ply of floss.

WILLDLIFE

ANCHOR		DMC	
002	·	000	White
403	■	310	Black
013	♥	349	Dark coral
009	╱	352	Pale coral
217	☒	367	Pistachio
401	◉	413	Pewter
267	☆	470	Avocado
1040	▢	647	True beaver gray
891	⊞	676	Light old gold
886	▬	677	Pale old gold
926	⋮	712	Cream
326	★	720	Bittersweet
305	≡	725	Topaz
890	⊠	729	Medium old gold
316	◆	740	Dark tangerine
314	◉	741	Medium tangerine
307	✳	783	Christmas gold
162	▼	825	Bright blue
1041	⊞	844	Deep beaver gray
360	●	898	Coffee brown
269	▲	936	Pine green
355	✤	975	Golden brown
433	◈	996	Electric blue
397	S	3024	Brown gray
888	▶	3045	Yellow beige
928	‖	3761	Sky blue

ANCHOR		DMC	
BACKSTITCH			
403	╱	310	Black
150	╱	336	Navy
013	╱	349	Dark coral
217	╱	367	Pistachio
683	╱	500	Deep blue green
326	╱	720	Bittersweet
305	╱	725	Topaz
397	╱	3024	Brown gray
382	╱	3371	Black brown
STRAIGHT STITCH			
002	╱	000	White
BRAIDED TAIL			
1040	╱	647	True beaver gray
FRENCH KNOT			
002	●	000	White
403	●	310	Black
013	●	349	Dark coral
217	●	367	Pistachio
382	●	3371	Black brown
LAZY DAISY			
217	⬭	367	Pistachio

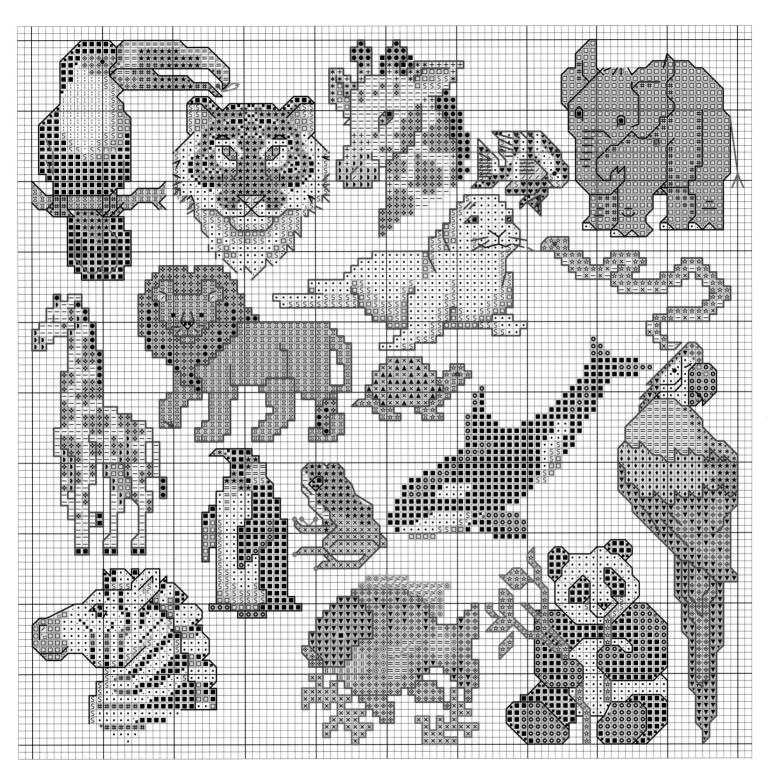

wildlife

pets

inspirations Feathered or furry, scaly or shell-topped, this group of animals is inspired by those special ones we call friends.

ideas

- Create a pet mat for your dog or cat by stitching the design on plastic canvas and finishing the edge with contrasting blanket stitches.
- Make a birdie bookmark in an evening by stitching a feathered friend on perforated plastic and finishing the edges with whipstitches.
- Stitch goldfish on a plain shower curtain, flopping the pattern occasionally, using waste canvas.

plate no. 52

pets

pets

We stitched the Pets cross-stitch plate, *opposite*, over two threads on 28-count Mushroom (#309) Lugana fabric. All cross-stitches are completed using two plies of cotton embroidery floss. All other stitches are completed using one ply of floss.

PETS

ANCHOR		DMC	
002	·	000	White
352	◆	300	Deep mahogany
1049	✕	301	Medium mahogany
403	■	310	Black
400	▢	317	True pewter
008	✳	353	Peach
310	◉	434	Chestnut
1045	▦	436	Tan
233	◎	451	Dark shell gray
232	☆	452	Medium shell gray
231	▤	453	Light shell gray
267	◍	470	Avocado
168	◰	597	Medium turquoise
167	◻	598	Light turquoise
324	⊠	721	Bittersweet
1022	♡	760	Salmon
359	●	801	Coffee brown
169	▲	806	Peacock blue
338	⊞	921	Copper
274	╱	928	Gray blue
1002	◯	977	Light golden brown
244	▨	987	Forest green
886	+	3047	Yellow beige
306	❖	3820	Straw
363	Ⓢ	3827	Pale golden brown

ANCHOR		DMC	
BACKSTITCH			
002	╱	000	White
352	╱	300	Deep mahogany
403	╱	310	Black
401	╱	413	Dark pewter
233	╱	451	Dark shell gray
169	╱	806	Peacock blue
338	╱	921	Copper
STRAIGHT STITCH			
1022	╱	760	Salmon
FRENCH KNOT			
002	●	000	White
403	●	310	Black
401	●	413	Dark pewter
1022	●	760	Salmon
306	●	3820	Straw

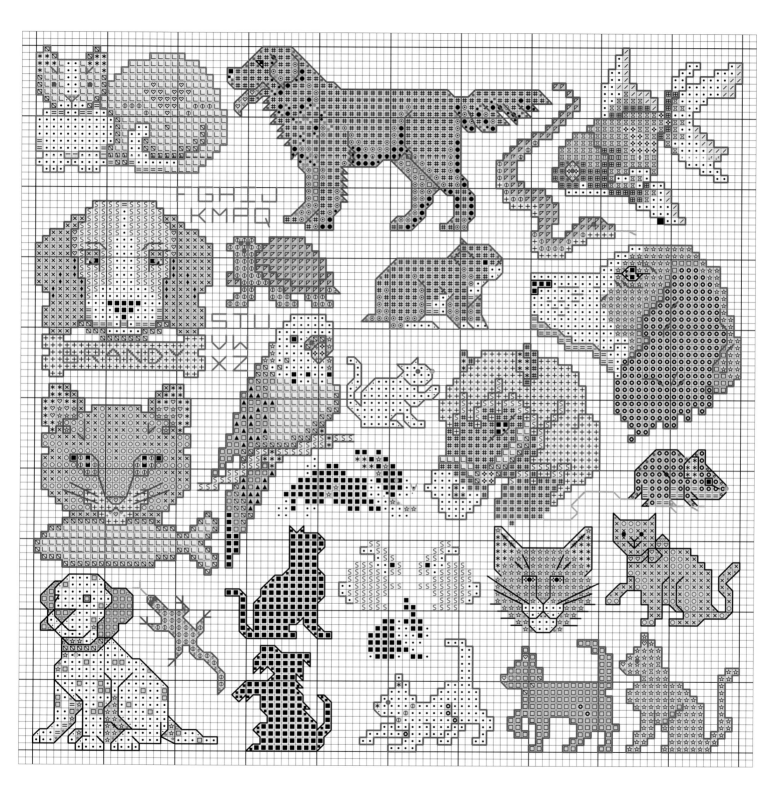

pets

farm & forest

inspirations
Inspired by animals that live in the woods or in pastures, these designs will bring out the animal lover in you.

ideas

- Stitch your favorite animal on a checkbook cover.
- Use waste canvas to stitch a trio of forest animals on the front of a sweatshirt.
- Stitch a parade of farm animals and frame it for any room of the house.

plate no. 53
farm and forest

farm & forest

instruction

We stitched the Farm and Forest cross-stitch plate, *opposite,* over two threads on 28-count Lavender (#559) Lugana fabric. All cross-stitches are completed using two plies of cotton embroidery floss. All other stitches are completed using one ply of floss.

FARM AND FOREST

ANCHOR		DMC
002	⋅	000 White
1049	☒	301 Medium mahogany
403	■	310 Black
148	⊞	311 Navy
400	▢	317 True pewter
399	⊞	318 Steel
1047	S	402 Pale mahogany
401	◉	413 Dark pewter
310	☆	434 Medium chestnut
1046	▽	435 Light chestnut
1045	△	436 Dark tan
832	⊙	612 Drab brown
903	◆	640 Beige gray
926	—	712 Cream
305	‖	725 True topaz
361	O	738 Light tan
1012	▱	754 Peach
882	♡	758 Terra-cotta
308	◩	782 Medium topaz
175	◇	794 Cornflower blue
144	L	800 Delft blue
045	♥	814 Dark garnet
043	✳	815 Medium garnet
360	▲	839 Beige brown
1041	✜	844 Beaver gray
944	▶	869 Hazel
360	◪	898 Coffee brown
205	◍	911 Emerald
204	☒	913 Nile green
1015	★	918 Dark red copper
1014	△	919 True red copper
338	▨	921 Copper
1035	⊞	930 Antique blue
1002	✶	977 Golden brown
1024	⦂	3328 Salmon
382	◓	3371 Black brown

ANCHOR		DMC
BACKSTITCH		
002	╱	000 White
310	╱	434 Medium chestnut
1041	╱	844 Beaver gray
382	╱	3371 Black brown
STRAIGHT STITCH		
308	╱	782 Medium topaz
205	╱	911 Emerald
FRENCH KNOT		
002	●	000 White
1041	●	844 Beaver gray
LAZY DAISY		
205	⬭	911 Emerald

farm and forest

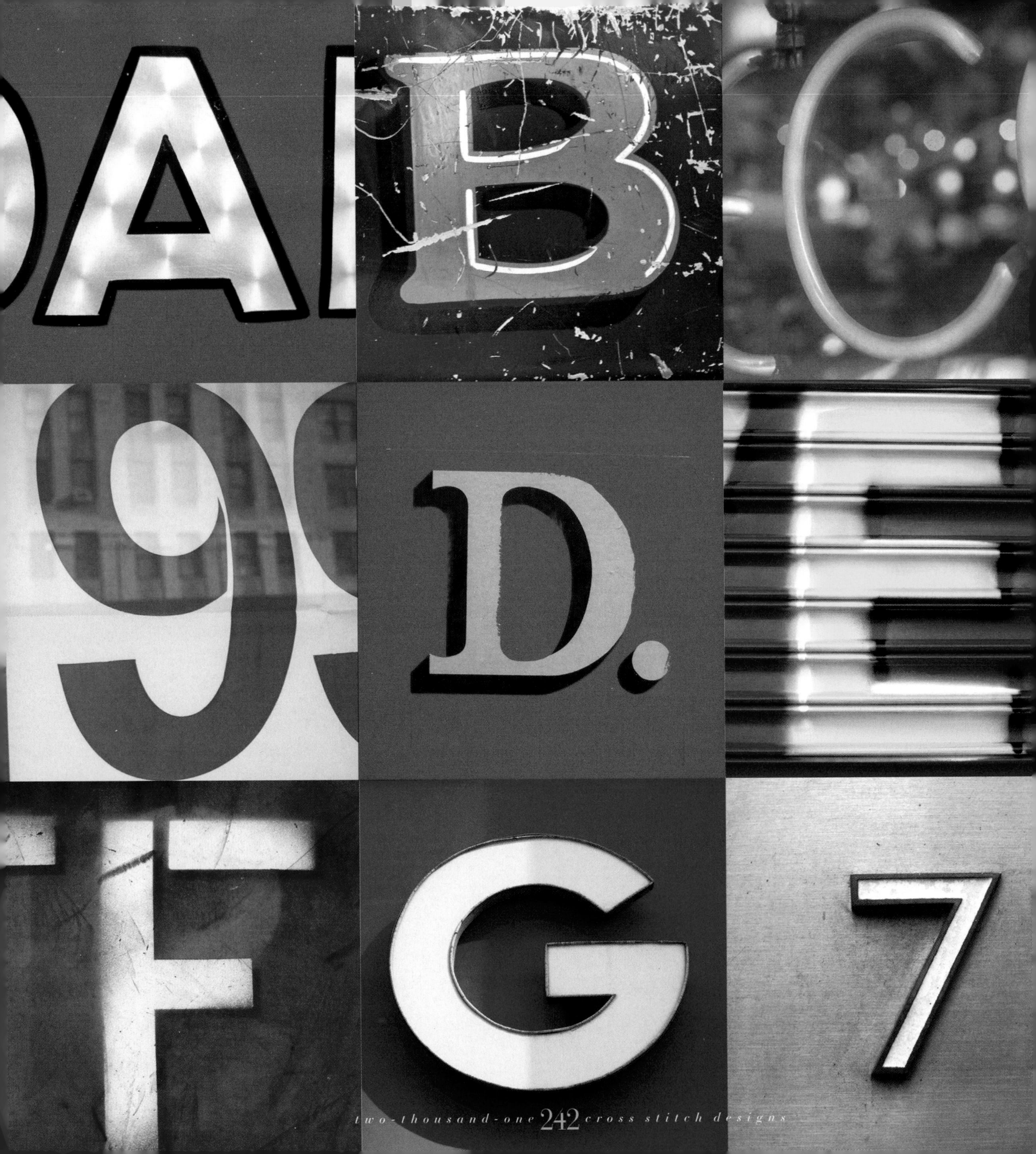
A
B
C
99
D.
F
G
7

The variety of styles of letters and numbers in this collection will inspire you to design your own cross-stitch projects. Perfect for samplers, monograms, and other personalized projects, these alphabets will be used again and again. To help you use these designs in your cross-stitch projects, turn to *pages 302–305* for help on how to design your own pieces using this fun-to-stitch assortment.

alphabets & numbers

pretty & simple

inspirations
Floral touches and elegant swirls inspire this assortment of sweet alphabets and numerals.

ideas

• Stitch newlyweds a set of floral monogrammed pillowcases using the alphabet with the tiny blooms.

• Use one of the small alphabets to stitch "Friends" vertically on a bookmark, then embellish with tiny floral or heart motifs.

• Use an alphabet with upper and lower case letters to stitch mom's favorite saying and give it to her on Mother's Day.

plate no. 54
pretty and simple

pretty & simple

instruction

We stitched the Pretty and Simple alphabet cross-stitch plate, *opposite*, over two threads on 28-count Mushroom (#309) Lugana fabric. All cross-stitches are completed using two plies of cotton embroidery floss. All other stitches are completed using one ply of floss.

PRETTY AND SIMPLE

ANCHOR		DMC	
895	⊙	223	Medium shell pink
289	⁄	307	Lemon
167	⊕	598	Medium turquoise
176	☒	793	Medium cornflower blue
175	⊟	794	Light cornflower blue
242	⊞	989	Forest green
068	▽	3687	True mauve
177	⊙	3807	True cornflower blue

ANCHOR		DMC	
BACKSTITCH			
897	⁄	221	Deep shell pink
069	⁄	3803	Dark mauve
779	⁄	3809	Dark turquoise

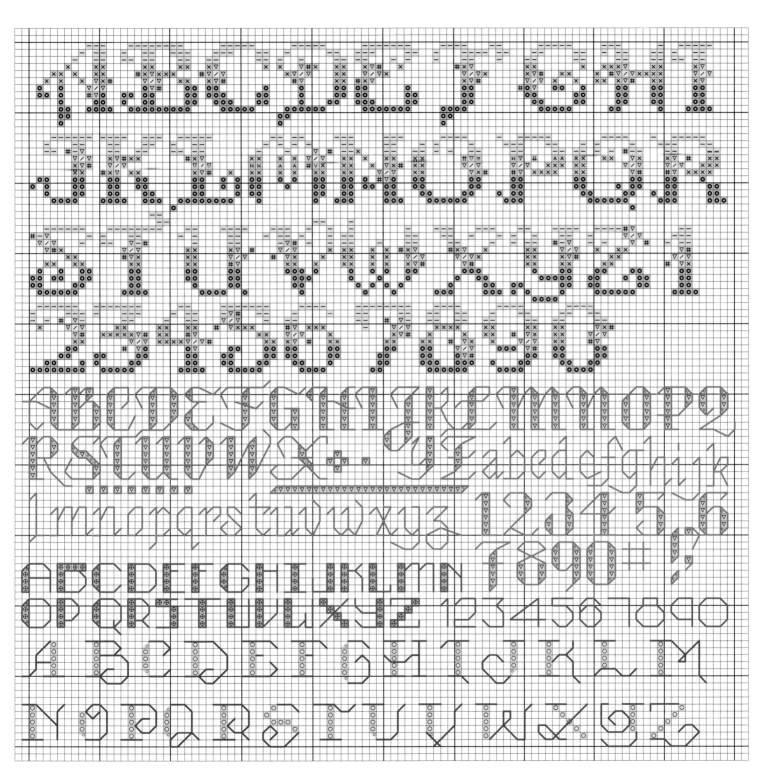

pretty and simple

country alphabets

inspirations

Nostalgic motifs and country colors inspire this grouping of alphabets that range from quick-stitch to cleverly detailed.

ideas

- Stitch a sampler using the large alphabet and mount in a barnwood frame.
- Use the three-color alphabet to personalize a man's handkerchief.
- Create your own Christmas sampler by combining the solid alphabet with some of your favorite motifs from *pages 88–125.*

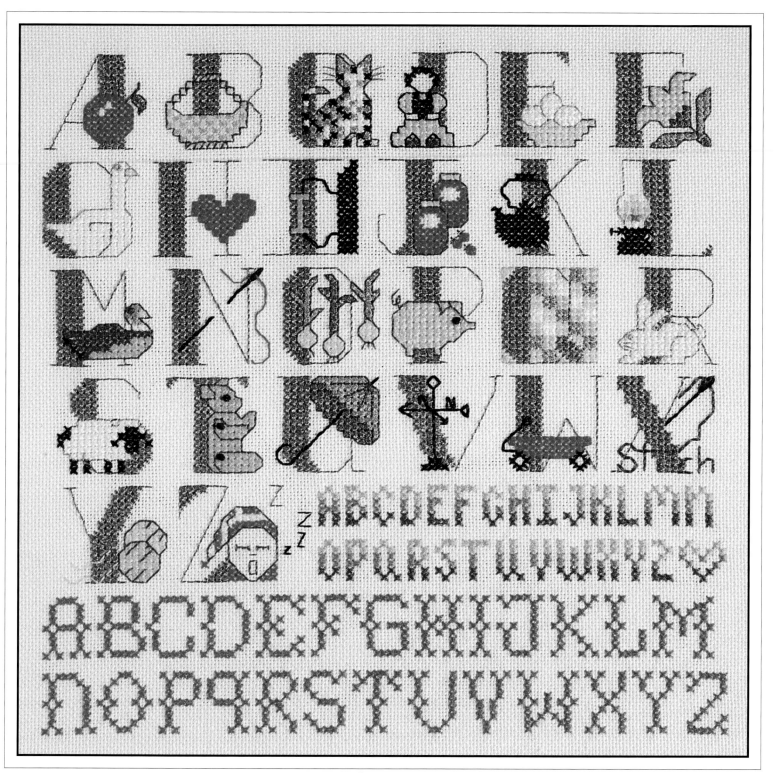

plate no. 55
country alphabets

country alphabets

instruction

We stitched the Country Alphabets cross-stitch plate, *opposite*, over two threads on 28-count Carnation Pink (#400) Jubilee fabric. All cross-stitches are completed using two plies of cotton embroidery floss. All other stitches are completed using one ply of floss.

COUNTRY ALPHABETS

ANCHOR		DMC
002	⋅	000 White
403	■	310 Black
978	☒	322 Navy
235	⊙	414 Steel
310	✳	434 Chestnut
1045	☐	436 Tan
307	▽	783 Christmas gold
013	◉	817 Coral
380	●	838 Beige brown
360	◆	898 Coffee brown
258	▲	904 Parrot green
243	⊞	988 Forest green
036	−	3326 Rose
069	◎	3803 Mauve
874	Ⅰ	3822 Straw

ANCHOR		DMC
BACKSTITCH		
403	╱	310 Black
978	╱	322 Navy
235	╱	414 Steel
307	╱	783 Christmas gold
013	╱	817 Coral
380	╱	838 Beige brown
258	╱	904 Parrot green
036	╱	3326 Rose
874	╱	3822 Straw
STRAIGHT STITCH		
235	╱	414 Steel
FRENCH KNOT		
403	●	310 Black
235	●	414 Steel
380	●	838 Beige brown
LAZY DAISY		
403	◊	310 Black

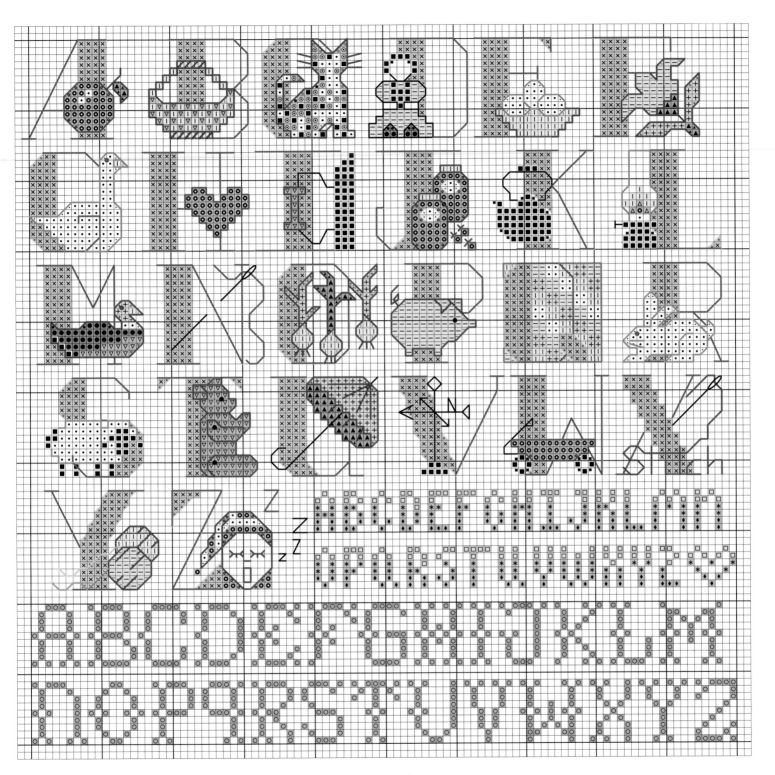

country alphabets

R back to school

inspirations
Bringing back memories of good ol' school days, this alphabet is inspired by basic school supplies.

ideas
- Stitch the entire alphabet and frame the piece with rulers or pieces of a yardstick.
- Create a treasured gift for a teacher by stitching his or her first initial and insert into a paperweight.
- Use this alphabet to stitch "Dad's Shop" to hang over his workbench.

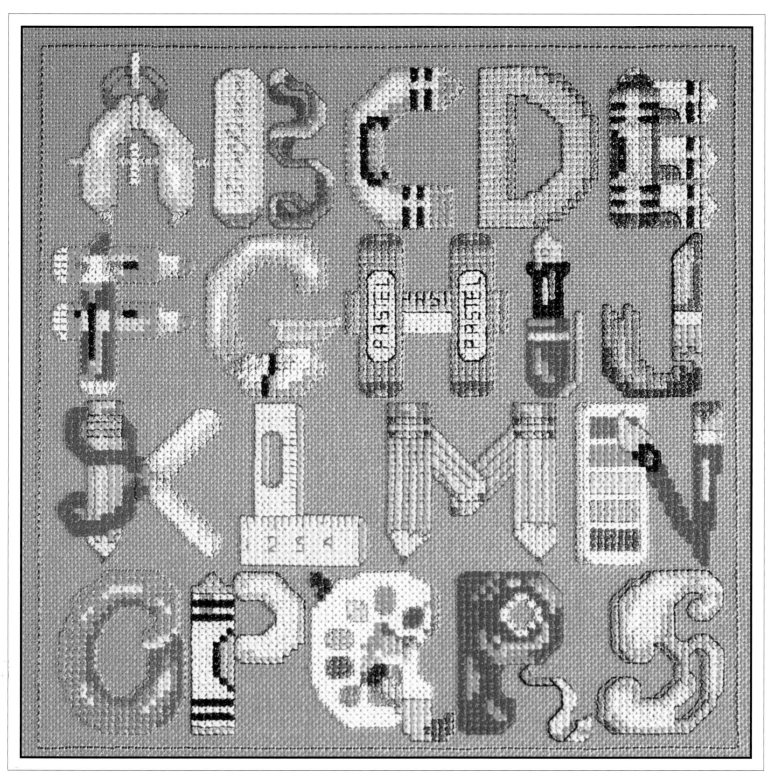

plate no. 56
back to school

back to school

instruction

We stitched the Back to School alphabet cross-stitch plate, *opposite,* over two threads on 28-count Tobacco (#308) Cashel Linen fabric. All cross-stitches are completed using two plies of cotton embroidery floss. All other stitches are completed using one ply of floss. We stitched a single blue line around this plate to show a quick and effective border detail that you can add before framing, if desired. The designs for the last of the Back to School alphabet can be found on *pages 256– 259.*

BACK TO SCHOOL

ANCHOR		DMC
002	⊡	000 White
403	■	310 Black
400	⊞	317 Pewter
399	☐	318 Steel
9046	◉	321 Christmas red
1047	Ⅲ	402 Mahogany
098	⊕	553 Medium violet
096	▷	554 Light violet
334	◑	606 Orange red
923	◆	699 Dark Christmas green
226	◉	702 Light Christmas green
256	△	704 Chartreuse
303	⊕	742 Tangerine
302	▽	743 True yellow
301	Ⅱ	744 Medium yellow
158	◠	747 Light sky blue
234	◲	762 Pearl gray
259	◿	772 Loden
128	⠿	775 Baby blue
133	▲	796 Royal blue
131	⊖	798 Dark Delft blue
130	◇	809 True Delft blue
043	♥	815 Garnet
378	▣	841 True beige brown
388	▽	842 Light beige brown
360	▼	898 Coffee brown
089	◤	917 Plum
188	⊛	943 Dark aqua
330	✳	947 Burnt orange
186	◹	959 Medium aqua
075	⊞	962 Rose pink
410	●	995 Dark electric blue
433	✕	996 Medium electric blue
059	◈	3350 Deep dusty rose
074	◎	3354 Light dusty rose
087	✴	3607 Dark fuchsia
085	♡	3609 Light fuchsia
928	◳	3761 Medium sky blue

ANCHOR		DMC
BACKSTITCH		
403	╱	310 Black
400	╱	317 Pewter
9046	╱	321 Christmas red
923	╱	699 Dark Christmas green
043	╱	815 Garnet
360	╱	898 Coffee brown
188	╱	943 Dark aqua
410	╱	995 Dark electric blue

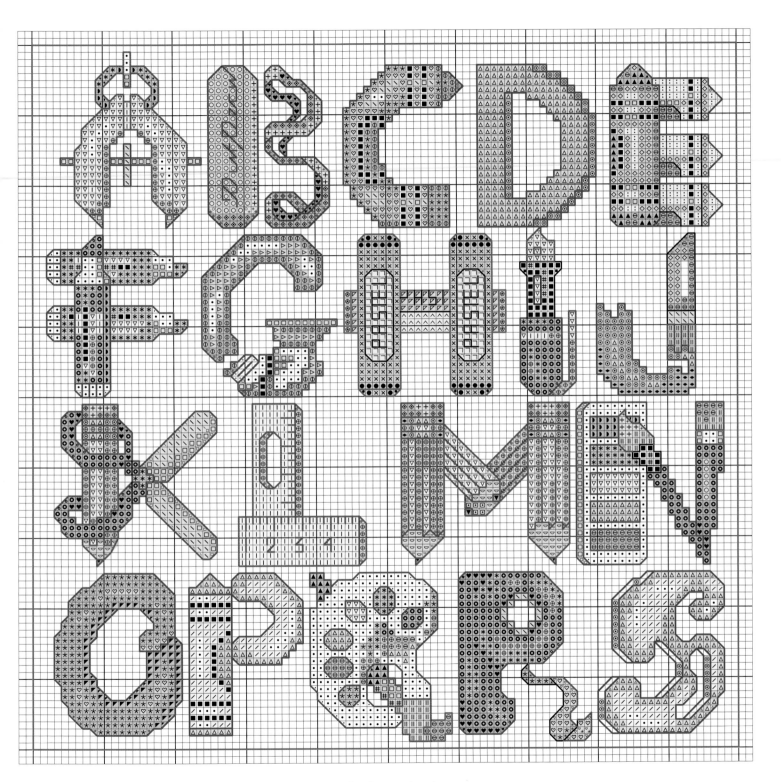

back to school

pencil alphabet

inspirations

Inspired by the most common writing tool, the pencil, this alphabet bends the rules to make lighthearted letters.

ideas

- Stitch a personalized drawstring bag to keep a collection of pencils.
- Treat a favorite teacher to a paperweight stitched with her initials.
- Stitch "Hello" on perforated paper to send greetings to a school chum.

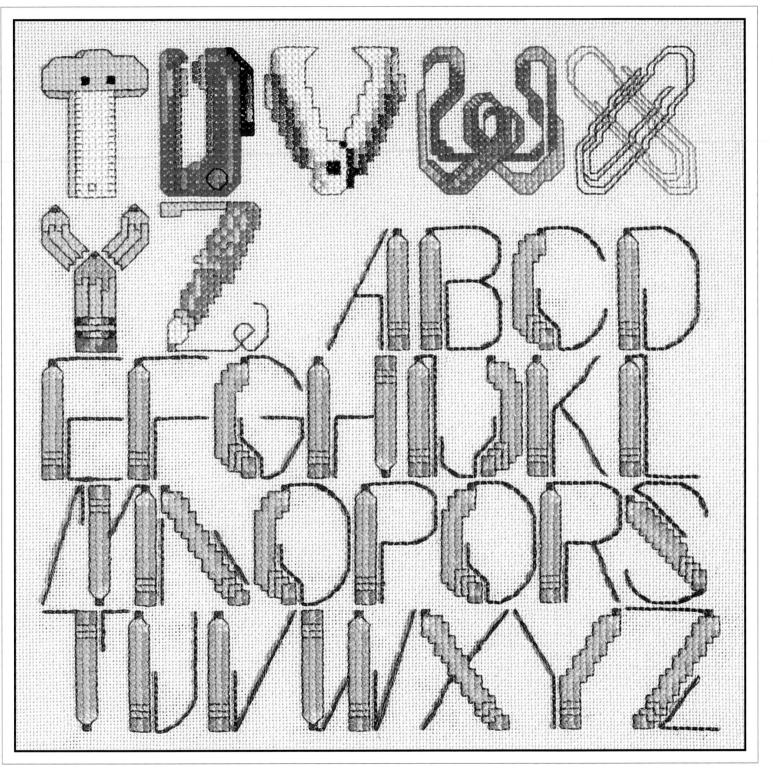

plate no. 57
pencil alphabet

pencil alphabet

instruction

We stitched the Pencil Alphabet cross-stitch plate, *opposite*, over two threads on 28-count Ice Blue (#550) Jubilee fabric. All cross-stitches are completed using two plies of cotton embroidery floss. All other stitches are completed using one ply of floss unless otherwise noted in the color key. The designs for the first section of the Back to School alphabet can be found on *pages 252–255.*

PENCIL ALPHABET

ANCHOR		DMC
002	•	000 White
403	■	310 Black
400	⊞	317 Pewter
399	▢	318 Steel
9046	◉	321 Christmas red
5975	✛	356 Medium terra-cotta
098	◐	553 Violet
334	◗	606 Orange red
900	⊟	648 Light beaver gray
923	◆	699 Dark Christmas green
226	◉	702 Light Christmas green
303	⊕	742 Tangerine
302	▽	743 Yellow
882	◖	758 Light terra-cotta
259	╱	772 Loden
307	◆	783 Christmas gold
043	♥	815 Garnet
378	▣	841 True beige brown
388	▽	842 Light beige brown
1041	☒	844 Deep beaver gray
360	▼	898 Coffee brown
330	✳	947 Burnt orange
4146	—	950 Rose beige
075	⊞	962 Rose pink
410	●	995 Dark electric blue
433	✕	996 Medium electric blue
059	◈	3350 Dusty rose
087	✶	3607 Dark fuchsia
085	♡	3609 Light fuchsia
928	▯	3761 Sky blue

ANCHOR		DMC
BACKSTITCH		
403	╱	310 Black
400	╱	317 Pewter
9046	╱	321 Christmas red
923	╱	699 Dark Christmas green
043	╱	815 Garnet
1041	╱	844 Deep beaver gray (1X)
1041	╱	844 Deep beaver gray (4X)
360	╱	898 Dark coffee brown
410	╱	995 Dark electric blue
087	╱	3607 Dark fuchsia

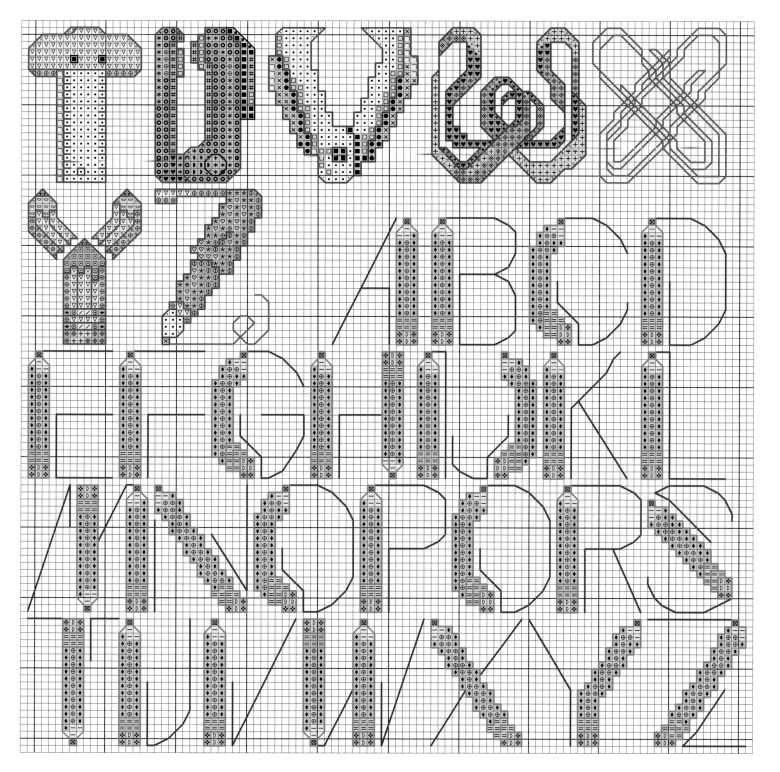

pencil alphabet

victorian ivy

inspirations The elegant
lines and colors of the Victorian style
inspire this dainty alphabet stitched in
two shades of blue.

ideas

- Stitch a lovely message such as "Sleep Well" to adorn a guest room wall or pillow sham.
- Make and personalize a glasses case from yellow cross-stitch fabric using initials from this alphabet.
- Delete the ivy for a quick-stitch alphabet that requires no backstitching.

plate no. 58
victorian ivy

victorian ivy

instruction

We stitched the Victorian Ivy alphabet cross-stitch plate, *opposite*, over two threads on 28-count Carnation Pink (#400) Jubilee fabric. All cross-stitches are completed using two plies of cotton embroidery floss. All other stitches are completed using one ply of floss. The design for the end of the Victorian Ivy alphabet can be found on *pages 264–267*.

VICTORIAN IVY		
ANCHOR	**DMC**	
136	☒	799 Delft blue
BACKSTITCH		
132	╱	797 Royal blue

victorian ivy

handsome alphabets

inspirations

Solid bold colors
inspire these versatile
alphabets that
come in all shapes
and sizes.

ideas

- Add a monogram to the lapel of a man's bathrobe using the large block lettering, stacked vertically.
- Stitch a mini sampler using the small block lettering and your favorite tiny motifs.
- Create a "Tooth Fairy Pillow" by using the delicate script lettering and a sweet heart or ribbon design.

plate no. 59
handsome alphabets

handsome alphabets

instruction

We stitched the Handsome Alphabets cross-stitch plate, *opposite*, over two threads on 28-count Maize (#226) Annabelle fabric. All cross-stitches are completed using two plies of cotton embroidery floss. All other stitches are completed using one ply of floss. The designs for the first section of the Victorian Ivy alphabet can be found on *pages 260–263*.

HANDSOME ALPHABETS		
ANCHOR	DMC	
310	▦	780 Topaz
136	☒	799 Delft blue
089	◉	917 Plum
187	◈	958 Aqua

ANCHOR	DMC	
BACKSTITCH		
099	╱	552 Violet
310	╱	780 Topaz
132	╱	797 Royal blue
089	╱	917 Plum
FRENCH KNOT		
099	●	552 Violet

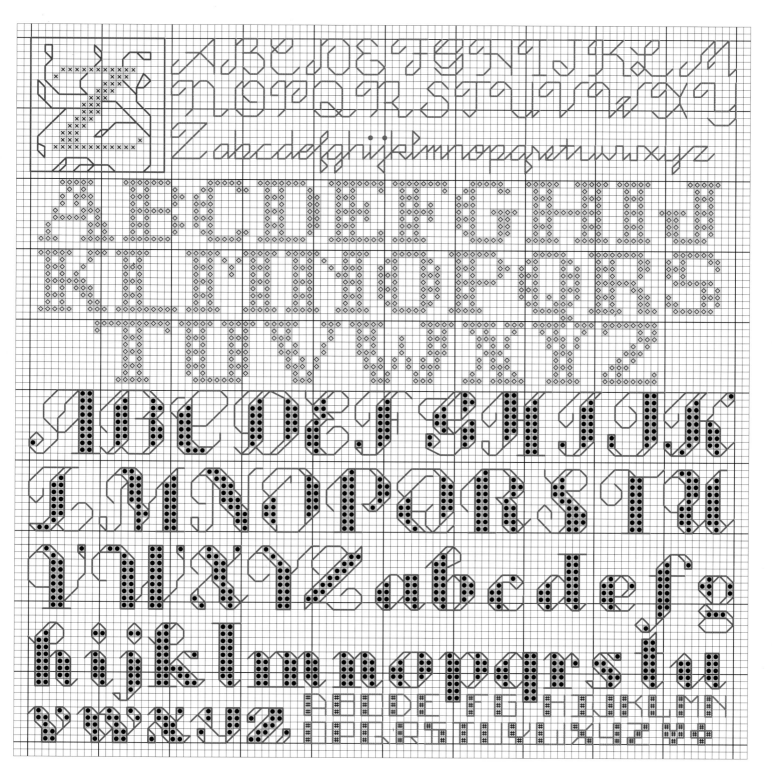

handsome alphabets

quick & script

inspirations
Letters with scroll-like touches inspire this pair of alphabets that stitch up quickly using only a few colors of floss.

ideas

- Use the Quick alphabet to personalize a child's school bag.
- Make "His" and "Hers" towels using the Script lettering to stitch on banding (adding appropriate motifs on each end of lettering) and attach to a bath towel two inches from the end.
- Create a sampler by combining the Quick alphabet with favorite mini motifs.

plate no. 60
quick and script

quick & script

instruction

We stitched the Quick and Script alphabets cross-stitch plate, *opposite*, over two threads on Maize 28-count (#226) Annabelle fabric. All cross-stitches are completed using two plies of cotton embroidery floss. All other stitches are completed using one ply of floss.

QUICK AND SCRIPT

ANCHOR		DMC
109	◎	209 Lavender
258	☒	904 Parrot green

BACKSTITCH

100	╱	327 Antique violet

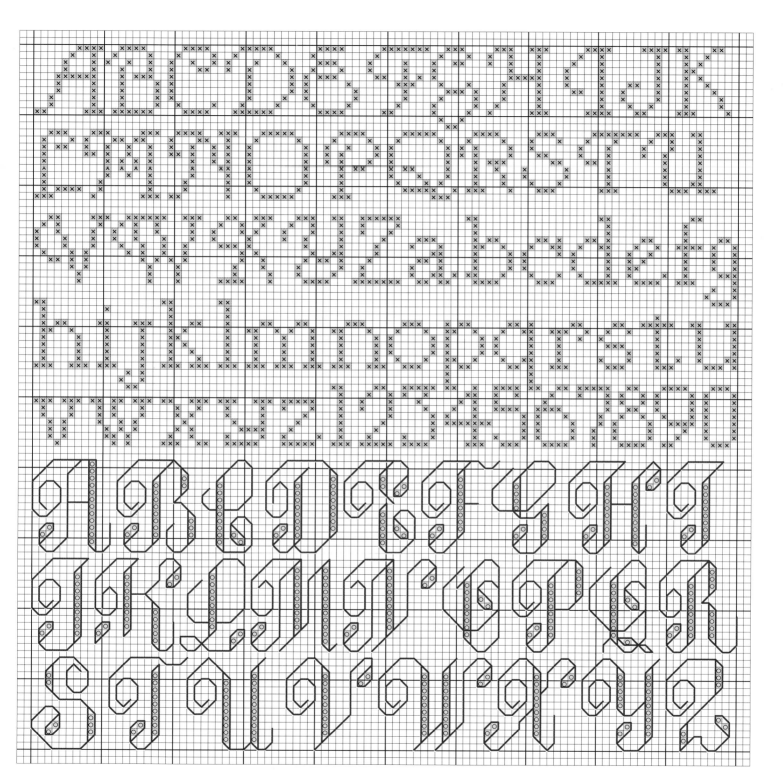

quick and script

playful alphabets

Inspired by baby
toys, accessories,
and curly Q's—these
fun-loving letters and
numbers will add a playful
touch to your cross-stitch projects.

ideas

- Stitch a bib with baby's name
  and the words "choo...choo" using
  the train alphabet.
- Add "Granny's Brag Book" to a
  fabric photograph book cover.
- Personalize a diaper bag using
  the safety pin alphabet.

plate no. 61
playful alphabets

playful alphabets

instruction

We stitched the Playful Alphabets cross-stitch plate, *opposite,* over two threads on 28-count Lavender (#559) Lugana fabric. All cross-stitches are completed using two plies of cotton embroidery floss. All other stitches are completed using one ply of floss.

PLAYFUL ALPHABETS

ANCHOR		DMC
110	⊖	208 Lavender
9046	◉	321 Christmas red
062	╱	603 Cranberry
295	▽	726 Topaz
178	✕	791 Cornflower blue
136	◇	799 Delft blue
205	◉	911 Emerald
186	▣	959 Aqua
298	✳	972 Canary
1028	✚	3685 Mauve
035	▢	3705 Watermelon

BACKSTITCH

401	╱	413 Pewter
178	╱	791 Cornflower blue
1028	╱	3685 Mauve

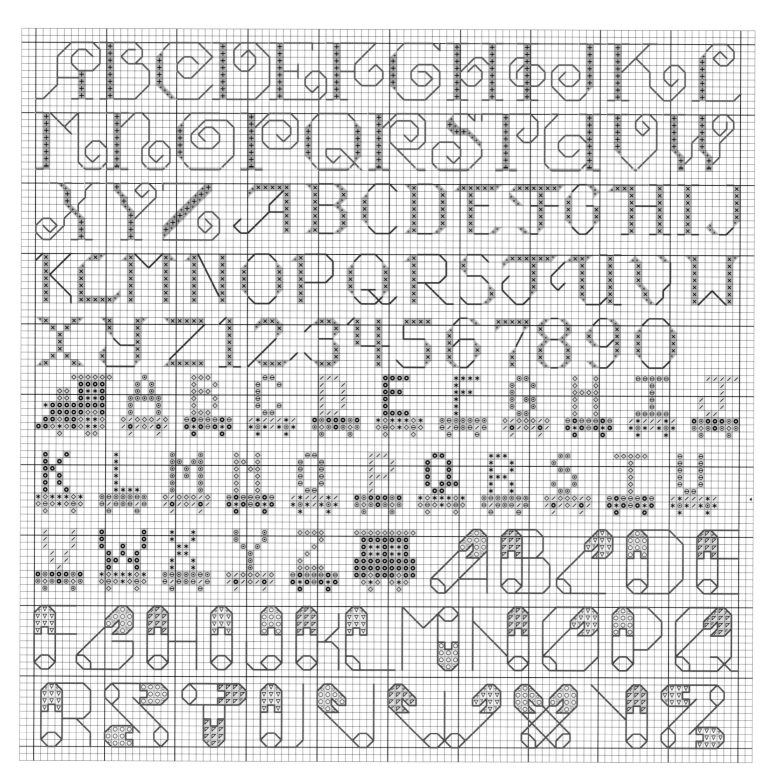

playful alphabets

G bold alphabets

inspirations Inspired by simple lines and a pair of primary colors, these two alphabets stitch up easily using only cross-stitches.

ideas

- Stitch the first letter of your last name to personalize a case for sunglasses. Add French knot polka-dots in the background.
- Use the star motif to add a patriotic touch to Fourth of July picnic napkins and napkin rings.
- Personalize a Christmas stocking cuff using the script alphabet.

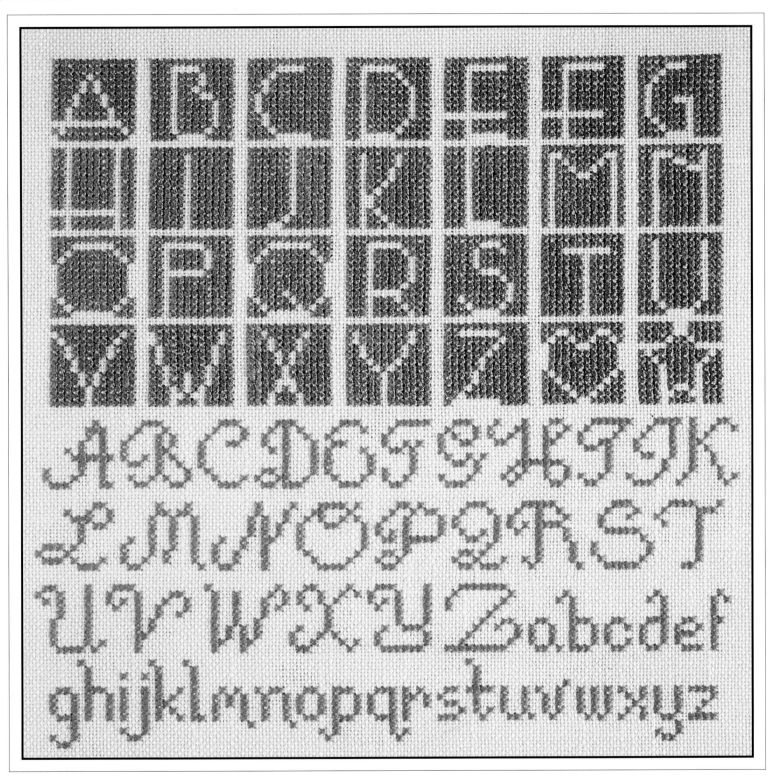

plate no. 62
bold alphabets

bold alphabets

instruction

We stitched the Bold Alphabets cross-stitch plate, *opposite*, over two threads on 28-count Maize (#226) Annabelle fabric. All cross-stitches are completed using two plies of cotton embroidery floss.

BOLD ALPHABETS		
ANCHOR		DMC
177	☒	792 Cornflower blue
069	⊙	3803 Mauve

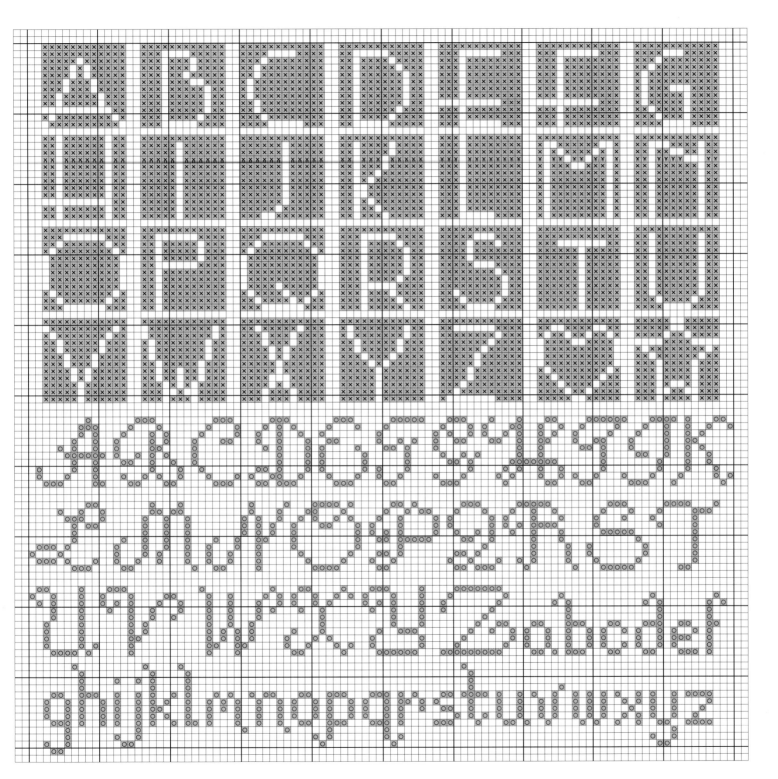

bold alphabets

Our daily routines, filled with hard work and fun play, are captured in cross-stitch in this exciting chapter. Designed for children and adults, these motifs relate to many of the ways we make a living as well as our leisure time activities. We hope these designs delight you and fulfill many happy hours of stitching.

sports, professions, & pastimes

needlework

inspirations

From cross-stitch to quilting, knitting to sewing, favorite techniques and accessories inspired these designs for needlework enthusiasts.

ideas

- Make a scissors case by stitching the large scissors on the front side of the case.
- Stitch the patchwork design on plastic canvas to make a one-of-a-kind belt.
- Stitch the heart design on perforated paper to make a special "thinking of you" card for a fellow stitcher.

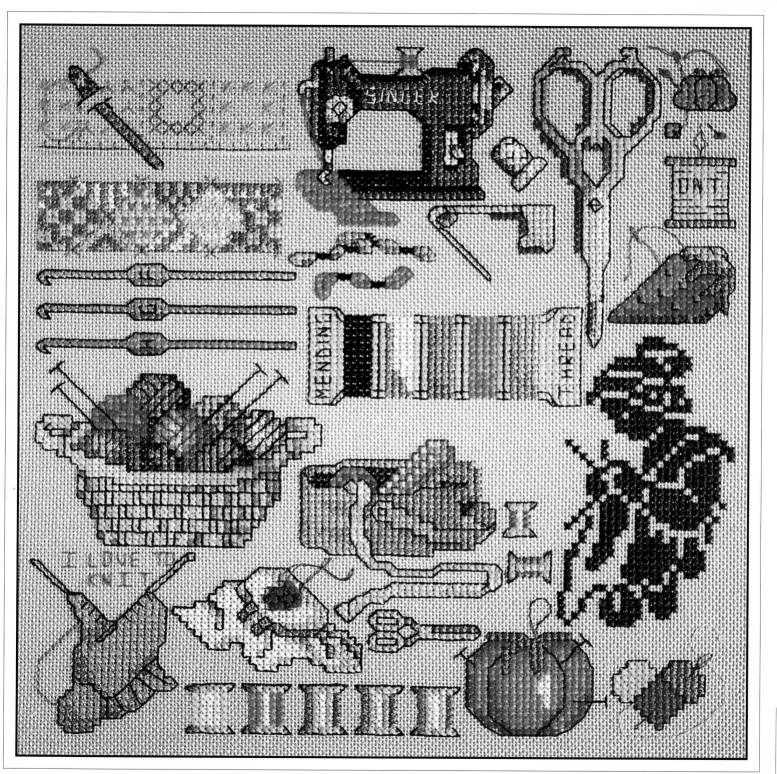

plate no. 63
needlework

needlework

instruction

We stitched the Needlework cross-stitch plate, *opposite*, over two threads on 28-count Wedgewood (#501) Lugana fabric. All cross-stitches are completed using two plies of cotton embroidery floss. All other stitches are completed using one ply of floss.

NEEDLEWORK

ANCHOR		DMC	
002	·	000	White
403	■	310	Black
399	+	318	Steel
150	◆	336	Navy
011	⊠	350	Medium coral
010	○	351	Light coral
398	−	415	Light pearl gray
374	☆	420	Hazel
267	◙	469	Avocado
683	⊞	500	Blue green
1041	▱	535	Ash gray
099	▼	552	Dark violet
096	⊟	554	Light violet
8581	⊕	646	Medium beaver gray
900	♡	648	Light beaver gray
891	∧	676	Light old gold
886	L	677	Pale old gold
295	⦂	726	Topaz
300	‖	745	Yellow
234	S	762	Pale pearl gray
307	△	783	Christmas gold
176	☐	793	Medium cornflower blue
175	◇	794	Light cornflower blue
013	♥	817	Deep coral
380	●	838	Beige brown
897	⋈	902	Garnet
268	◐	3345	Hunter green
264	✳	3348	Yellow green
074	I	3354	Dusty rose
068	◈	3687	True mauve
069	★	3803	Dark mauve
077	⊠	3807	True cornflower blue
877	▶	3815	Dark celadon green
876	⊞	3816	True celadon green
305	⊙	3821	True straw
874	∾	3822	Light straw

ANCHOR		DMC	
BACKSTITCH			
002	╱	000	White
403	╱	310	Black
150	╱	336	Navy
011	╱	350	Medium coral
267	╱	469	Avocado
683	╱	500	Blue green
1041	╱	535	Ash gray
099	╱	552	Dark violet
295	╱	726	Topaz
013	╱	817	Deep coral
897	╱	902	Garnet
382	╱	3371	Black brown
069	╱	3803	Dark mauve
177	╱	3807	True cornflower blue
FRENCH KNOT			
013	●	817	Deep coral (2X)
897	●	902	Garnet (2X)
RUNNING STITCH			
267	− −	469	Avocado
069	− −	3803	Dark mauve
LAZY DAISY			
1041	✐	535	Ash gray
SMYRNA CROSS			
307	✳	783	Christmas gold

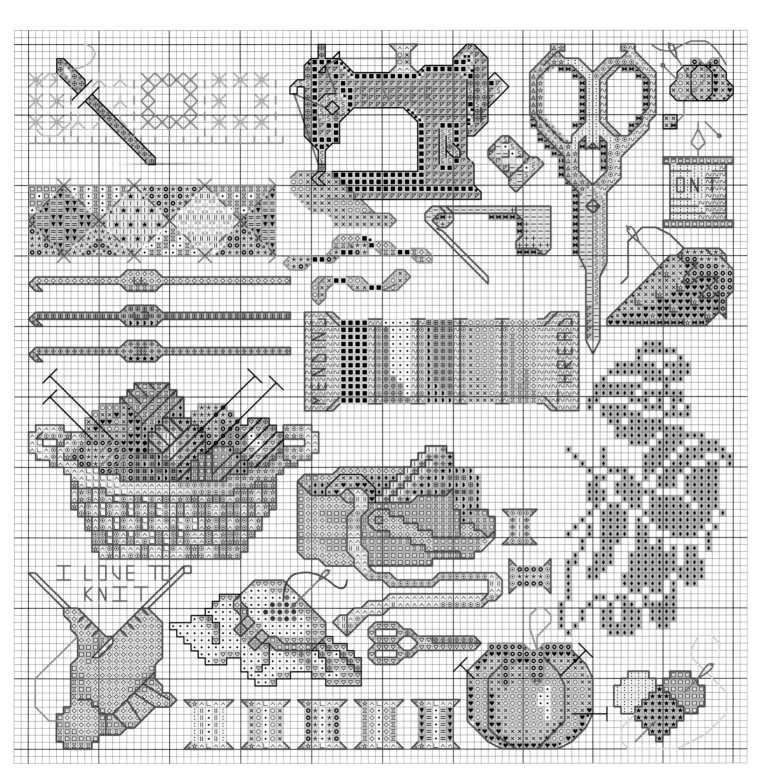

needlework

sports & hobbies

inspirations
Leisure-time hobbies and thrilling spectator sports were the inspiration for this "I'd rather be" selection of designs.

ideas

- Stitch sports motifs on fabric to cover a scrapbook or photo album for a sporty youth.
- Stitch a paint palette pin on perforated plastic.
- Make button covers stitched with the handsome horse-and-rider design.

plate no. 64
sports and hobbies

sports & hobbies

instruction

We stitched the Sports and Hobbies cross-stitch plate, *opposite,* over two threads on 28-count Mint Green (#621) Jubilee fabric. All cross-stitches are completed using two plies of cotton embroidery floss. All other stitches are completed using one ply of floss.

SPORTS AND HOBBIES

ANCHOR		DMC
002	·	000 White
403	■	310 Black
979	◆	312 Navy
400	☐	317 Pewter
399	⊞	318 Steel
977	⊙	334 Baby blue
1025	♥	347 Salmon
011	☒	350 Coral
217	☆	367 Medium pistachio
214	◇	368 Light pistachio
398	─	415 Pearl gray
358	◙	433 Dark chestnut
310	△	434 Medium chestnut
1045	⌂	436 Dark tan
362	‖	437 Medium tan
683	#	500 Blue green
8581	⊕	646 Medium beaver gray
900	♡	648 Light beaver gray
886	∟	677 Pale old gold
256	▽	704 Chartreuse
890	⊠	729 Medium old gold
302	⁚	743 Yellow
308	⊠	782 Topaz
359	▲	801 Coffee brown
944	⋈	869 Hazel
1015	★	918 Dark red copper
1014	◈	919 True red copper
338	⊘	921 Copper
868	⏟	3779 Terra-cotta
278	S	3819 Moss green

ANCHOR		DMC
BACKSTITCH		
002	╱	000 White
403	╱	310 Black
979	╱	312 Navy
399	╱	318 Steel
977	╱	334 Baby blue
1025	╱	347 Salmon
1014	╱	919 True red copper
338	╱	921 Copper
382	╱	3371 Black brown
236	╱	3799 Charcoal
877	╱	3815 Celadon green
FRENCH KNOT		
977	●	334 Baby blue
1025	●	347 Salmon
382	●	3371 Black brown

sports and hobbies

professions

inspirations
A sampling of popular professions inspired this collection of cross-stitch designs.

ideas

- Bring smiles to a favorite teacher by stitching a bookmark or a glasses case.
- Stitch the words "little pilot," using the alphabets on *pages 242–279*, along with the plane design for a toddler's bib.
- Stitch the chef on a cookbook cover.

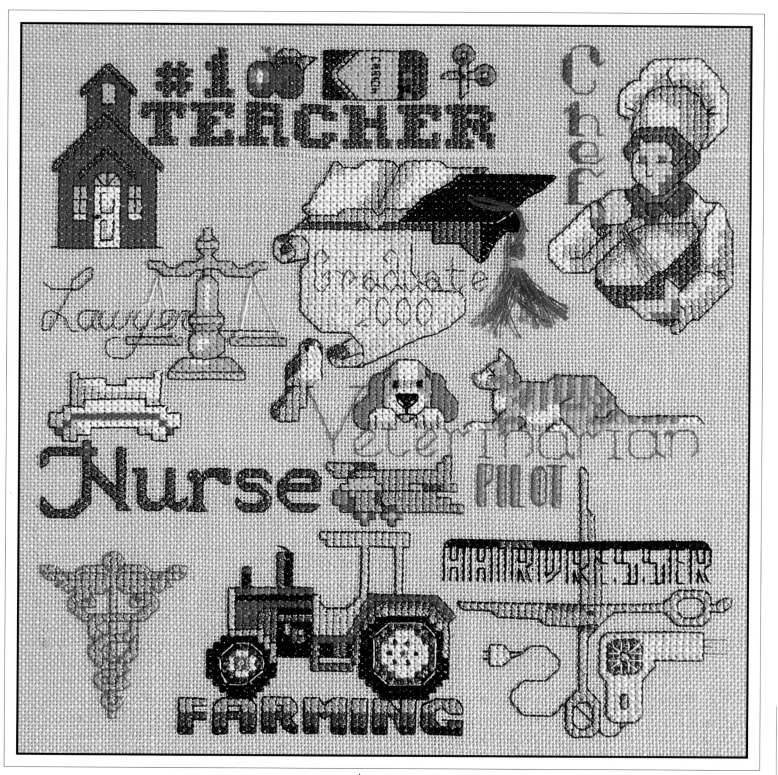

professions

instruction

We stitched the Professions cross-stitch plate, *opposite*, over two threads on 28-count Sand (#322) Cashel Linen fabric. All cross-stitches are completed using two plies of cotton embroidery floss. All other stitches are completed using one ply of floss.

PROFESSIONS

ANCHOR		DMC
387	☑	Ecru
002	·	000 White
1049	☒	301 Mahogany
403	■	310 Black
400	⊙	317 Pewter
399	⊞	318 Steel
118	☐	340 Periwinkle
010	▽	351 Light coral
398	⊟	415 Pearl gray
358	◉	433 Chestnut
228	☆	700 Christmas green
326	◆	720 Dark bittersweet
323	⊟	722 Light bittersweet
295	⋀	726 Topaz
361	◎	738 Light tan
885	Ⓢ	739 Pale tan
307	⊠	783 Christmas gold
177	▲	792 Cornflower blue
013	♥	817 Deep coral
218	●	890 Pistachio
204	⊕	913 Nile green
881	Ⅰ	945 Ivory
1002	☑	977 Golden brown
905	◣	3021 Brown gray
170	✛	3765 Deep peacock blue
167	♡	3766 Light peacock blue
1015	▼	3777 Terra-cotta
305	⊕	3821 True straw
874	⌊	3822 Light straw

ANCHOR		DMC
BACKSTITCH		
403	╱	310 Black
400	╱	317 Pewter
398	╱	415 Pearl gray
830	╱	644 Light beige gray
177	╱	792 Cornflower blue
013	╱	817 Deep coral
218	╱	890 Pistachio
089	╱	917 Plum
360	╱	3031 Mocha
170	╱	3765 Deep peacock blue
236	╱	3799 Charcoal
STRAIGHT STITCH		
118	╱	340 Periwinkle
295	╱	726 Topaz
SATIN STITCH		
403	╱	310 Black
FRENCH KNOT		
400	●	317 Pewter
010	●	351 Light coral
398	●	415 Pearl gray
295	●	726 Topaz
089	●	917 Medium plum
360	●	3031 Mocha
236	●	3799 Charcoal
TASSEL		
013	╱	817 Deep coral wrapped with
298	╱	972 Canary

professions

Whether you are a beginner or an advanced stitcher, the following pages of cross-stitch basics will help you get started by explaining the best ways to secure your first piece of floss, make your stitches, and complete your project like a pro. Plus, you'll become familiar with the latest materials and tips from expert stitchers, all presented here to help you cross-stitch with perfection.

cross-stitch basics

cross-stitch basics getting started

Choose the desired color of floss. Cut the floss into a 15- to 18-inch length strand and separate all six plies. Recombine the number of plies as indicated in the project instructions and thread into a blunt-tipped needle.

basic cross-stitch
Make one cross-stitch for each symbol on the chart. For horizontal rows, stitch the first diagonal of each stitch in the row.

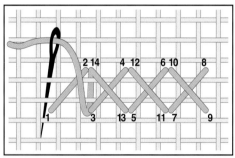

basic cross-stitch in rows

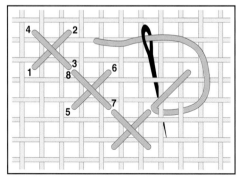

basic cross-stitch worked individually

Work back across the row, completing each stitch. On most linen and even-weave fabrics, stitches are usually worked over two threads as shown in the diagrams, *below left*. Each stitch fills one square on Aida cloth.

Cross-stitches also can be worked in the reverse direction; just remember to embroider the stitches uniformly. That is, always work so that the top half of the stitch is worked in the same direction.

how to secure thread at beginning
The most common way to secure the beginning tail of a piece of thread (floss) is to hold it under the first four or five stitches, *below*.

Or, you can use a waste knot, *right*. Thread needle and knot end of thread. Insert needle from right side of fabric, about 4 inches away from placement of first stitch. Bring needle up through fabric and work first series of stitches. When stitching is finished, turn piece to right side and clip the knot. Rethread needle with excess floss and push needle through to the wrong side of stitchery.

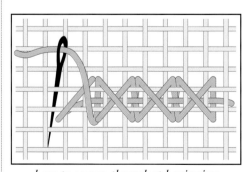

how to secure thread at beginning

When you work with two, four, or six plies of floss, use a loop knot. Cut half as many plies of thread, but make each one twice as long. Recombine plies, fold the strand in half, and thread all the ends into the needle. Work the first diagonal of the first stitch, then slip the needle through the loop formed by folding the thread.

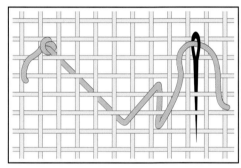

waste knot

how to secure thread at end
To finish, slip the threaded needle under the previously stitched threads on wrong side of the fabric for four or five stitches, weaving thread back and forth a few times. Clip the excess thread.

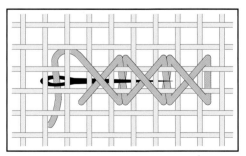

how to secure thread at end

half cross-stitches

A half cross-stitch is simply a single diagonal or half of a cross-stitch. Half cross-stitches usually are listed under a separate heading in the color key and are indicated on the chart by a diagonal colored line in the desired direction.

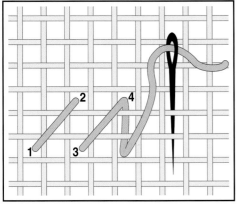

half cross-stitch

quarter and three-quarter stitches

Quarter and three-quarter cross-stitches are used to obtain rounded shapes in a design. On linen and even-weave fabrics, a quarter stitch extends from the corner to the center intersection of threads. To make quarter stitches on Aida cloth, you'll have to estimate the center of the square. Three-quarter stitches combine a quarter stitch with a half cross-stitch. Both of these stitches may slant in any direction.

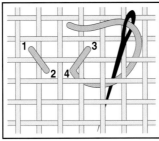

quarter cross-stitch

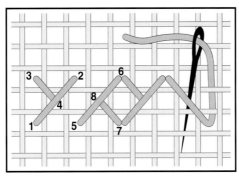

three-quarter cross-stitch

cross-stitches with beads

When beads are attached using a cross-stitch, work half cross-stitches, and then attach the beads on the return stitch.

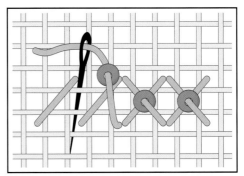

cross-stitch with bead

backstitches

Backstitches are added to define and outline the shapes in a design. For most cross-stitch projects, backstitches require only one ply of floss. On the color key, (2X) indicates two plies of floss, (3X) indicates three plies, etc.

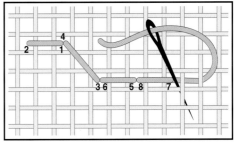

backstitch

fabric / needle / floss

FABRIC	NEEDLE SIZE	NUMBER OF PLIES
11-COUNT	24	THREE
14-COUNT	24-26	TWO OR THREE
18-COUNT	26	TWO
22-COUNT	26	ONE

cross-stitch basics materials

Counted cross-stitch has become a popular form of stitchery. Many stitchers like to work cross-stitch designs on different fabrics and use different threads than are specified in the projects. The following information will help you adapt the designs and projects in this book to meet your own needs.

cross-stitch fabrics

Counted cross-stitch can be worked on any fabric that will enable you to make consistently sized, even stitches.

Aida cloth is the most popular of all cross-stitch fabrics. Threads are woven in groups separated by tiny spaces. This creates a pattern of squares across the surface of the fabric and enables a beginning stitcher to easily identify where cross-stitches should be placed. Aida cloth is measured by squares per inch; 14-count Aida cloth has 14 squares per inch.

Aida cloth comes in many varieties. 100-percent cotton Aida cloth is available in thread counts 6, 8, 11, 14, 16, and 18. 14-count cotton Aida cloth is available in more than 60 colors. For beginners, white Aida cloth is available with a removable grid of prebasted threads.

Linen is considered to be the standard of excellence for experienced stitchers. The threads used to weave linen vary in thickness, giving linen fabrics a slightly irregular surface. When you purchase linen, remember that the thread count is measured by threads per inch, but most designs are worked over two threads, so 28-count linen will yield 14 stitches per inch. Linens are made in counts from 14 (seven stitches per inch) to 40.

Even-weave fabric also is worked over two threads. The popularity of cross-stitch has created a market for specialty fabrics for counted cross-stitch. They are referred to as even-weave fabrics because they are woven from threads with a consistent diameter, even though some of these fabrics are woven to create a homespun look. Most even-weave fabrics are counted like linen, by threads per inch, and worked over two threads.

Hardanger fabric can be used for very fine counted cross-stitch. The traditional fabric for the Norwegian embroidery of the same name has an over-two, under-two weave that produces 22 small squares per inch.

Needlepoint canvas is frequently used for cross-stitching, especially on clothing and other fabrics that are not suitable alone. Waste canvas is designed to unravel when dampened. It ranges in count from 6½ to 20 stitches per inch. Cross-stitches also can be worked directly on mono-needlepoint canvas. This is available in colors, and when the background is left unstitched, it can create an interesting effect.

Sweaters and other knits often are embellished with duplicate stitches from cross-stitch charts. Knit stitches are not square; they are wider than they are tall.

A duplicate-stitched design will appear broader and shorter.

Gingham or other checked fabrics can be used, but these "squares" may not be perfectly square, so a stitched design may seem taller and narrower than the chart.

Burlap fabric can easily be counted and stitched over as you would stitch a traditional counted-thread fabric.

types of needles

Blunt-pointed needles are best for working on most cross-stitch fabrics because they slide through holes and between threads without splitting or snagging the fibers. A large-eyed needle accommodates the bulk of embroidery threads. Many companies sell such needles labeled "cross-stitch," but they are identical to tapestry needles, blunt-tipped and large-eyed. The chart on *page 297* will guide you to the right size needle for most common fabrics. One exception to the blunt-tipped needle rule is waste canvas; use sharp embroidery needles to poke through that fabric.

Working with seed beads requires a very fine needle to slide through the holes. A #8 quilting needle, which is short with a tiny eye, and a long beading needle with its longer eye are readily available. Some shops carry short beading needles with a long eye.

threads for stitching

Most types of thread available for embroidery can be used for counted cross-stitch projects.

Six-ply cotton embroidery floss is available in the widest range of colors, including variegated ones. Six-ply floss is made to be separated easily into single or multiple plies for stitching. Instructions with each project in this book tell you how many plies to use. A greater number of plies will result in an embroidered piece that is rich or heavy; fewer plies will create a lightweight or fragile texture.

Rayon or silk floss is similar in weight to cotton floss, but the stitches have a greater sheen. Either thread can be exchanged with cotton floss, one ply for one ply, but because they have a "slicker" texture, they are slightly more difficult to use.

Pearl cotton is available in four sizes: #3, #5, #8, and #12 (#3 is thick; #12 is thin). It has an obvious twist and a high sheen.

Flower thread is a 100-percent cotton, matte-finish thread. A single strand of flower thread can be substituted for two plies of cotton embroidery floss.

Overdyed threads are being introduced on the market every day. Most of them have an irregularly variegated, one-of-a-kind appearance. Cotton floss, silk floss, flower thread, and pearl cotton weight threads are available in this form. All of them produce a soft shaded appearance without changing thread colors.

Specialty threads can add a distinctive look to cross-stitch. They range in weight from hair-fine blending filament, usually used with floss, to 1/8-inch-wide ribbon. They include numerous metallic threads, richly colored and textured threads, and fun-to-stitch, glow-in-the-dark threads.

Wool yarn, usually used for needlepoint or crewel embroidery, can be used for cross-stitch. Use one or two plies of three-ply Persian yarn. Select even-weave fabrics with fewer threads per inch when working cross-stitches in wool yarn.

Ribbon in silk, rayon, and polyester becomes an interesting texture for cross-stitching, especially in combination with flower-shaped stitches. Look for straight-grain and bias-cut ribbons in solid and variegated colors and in widths from 1/16 to 1 1/2 inches.

tips

preparing fabric

The edges of cross-stitch fabric take a lot of abrasion while a project is being stitched. There are many ways to keep fabric from fraying while you stitch.

The easiest and most widely available method is to bind the edges with masking tape. Because tape leaves a residue that's almost impossible to remove, it should be trimmed away after stitching is completed. All projects in this book that include tape in the instructions were planned with a large margin around the stitched fabric so the tape can be cut away.

There are some projects where you should avoid using masking tape. If a project does not allow for ample margins to trim away the tape, use one of these techniques: If you have a sewing machine readily available, zigzag stitching, serging, and narrow hemming are all neat and effective methods. Hand-overcasting also works well, but it is more time consuming.

Garments, table linens, towels, and other projects that will be washed on a regular basis when finished should be washed before stitching to avoid shrinkage later. Wash the fabric in the same manner you will wash the finished project.

preparing floss

Most cotton embroidery floss is colorfast and won't fade. A few bright colors, notably reds and greens, contain excess dye that could bleed onto fabrics if dampened. To remove the excess dye before stitching, gently slip off paper bands from floss and rinse each color in cool water until it runs clear. Then place floss on white paper towels to dry. If there is any color on the towels when the floss is dry, repeat the process. When dry, slip the paper bands back on the floss.

centering the design

Most of the projects in this book instruct you to begin stitching at the center of the chart and fabric. To find the center of a desired motif, find the horizontal and vertical centers of the motif. Where they intersect is the center of the design. If you are charting your own combination of designs, you find the center of the chart in the same manner.

To find the center of the fabric, fold it in half horizontally; baste along the fold. Then fold the fabric in half vertically; baste along the fold. The point where the basting intersects is the center. You can add additional basting lines every 10 or 20 rows to act as stitching guides.

cleaning your work

You may want to wash needlecraft pieces before mounting and framing them because the natural oils from your hands eventually will discolor the stitchery. Wash stitchery by hand in cool water using mild detergent. Rinse until the water is clear.

Do not wring or squeeze the needlecraft piece to get the water out. Hold the piece over the sink until dripping slows, then place flat on a clean terry-cloth towel, and roll tightly. Unroll and lay flat to dry.

pressing your work

Using a warm iron, press the cross-stitched fabric from the back before framing or finishing. If the piece has a lot of surface texture stitches, place it on a terry-cloth towel or other padded surface to press.

framing your design

For most purposes, omit glass when framing your cross-stitch. Moisture can build up between it and the stitchery, and sunlight is intensified by the glass. Both can cause damage to the fabric. If you must use glass, be sure to mat the piece so the stitchery does not touch the glass.

Now that you have hundreds of cross-stitch designs to choose from, how do you use them? What if you want to turn your stitched work of art into a bookmark, glasses case, or mini banner? The following pages will share pointers on combining motifs, how to center a design on fabric, and how to make it larger or smaller. These planning, stitching, and finishing suggestions will help you achieve success and may introduce you to new finishing techniques sure to enhance your cross-stitched works of art.

from start to finish

from start to finish

about our projects

All of the projects and patterns on *pages 314-329* have been selected because they work well with the mini cross-stitch designs in this book. All of the plates are stitched over two threads on 28-count fabric, meaning that each of the designs has 14 cross-stitches to the inch. As you can see from the Mini Banner sample pattern, *right*, the full-size patterns are also 14 squares to the inch to help in selecting designs to fit each pattern.

selecting designs to fit a pattern

Referring to the original chart you wish to stitch, count and record the stitch count. For instance, the "Joy" motif (see the example, *opposite*) that was selected to be stitched for the Mini Banner sample is 35 stitches wide by 15 stitches high (35w×15h). This will fit nicely into the 44w×60h dimensions of the Mini Banner pattern.

For a top border, the repetitive straight-stitch holly border was chosen from *page 99*. And for a striking design below the word "Joy" a sweet angel motif was selected from *page 107*.

After determining the stitch count of the chosen design(s), find the center of each design by dividing both the height and width by two. Draw arrows at the edge of the design, see diagram, *right*, to indicate the centers of your chosen designs. If using a pattern (such as our Mini Banner pattern) indicate the center of the pattern as well.

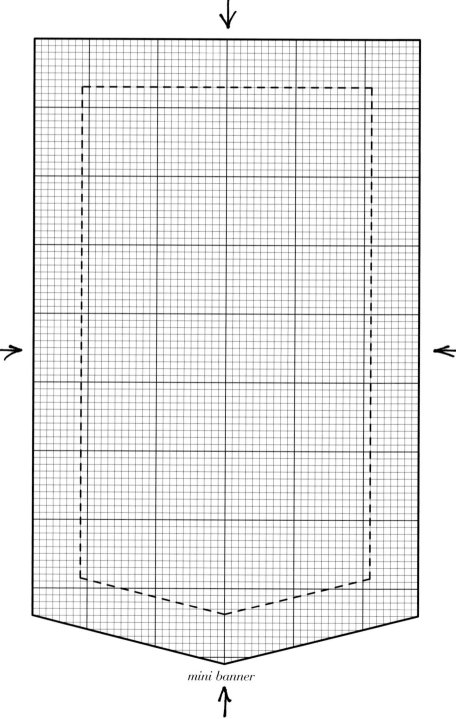

mini banner

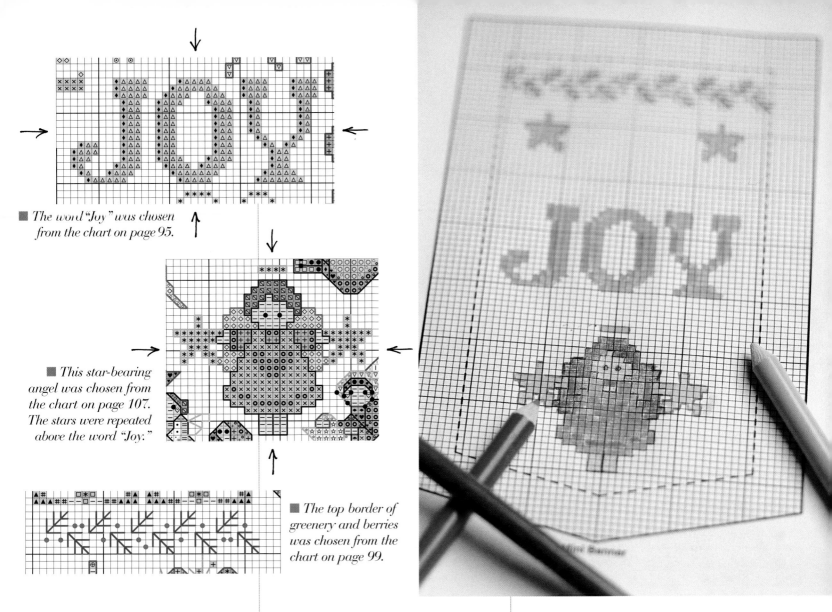

■ *The word "Joy" was chosen from the chart on page 95.*

■ *This star-bearing angel was chosen from the chart on page 107. The stars were repeated above the word "Joy."*

■ *The top border of greenery and berries was chosen from the chart on page 99.*

charting designs

To be certain your selected cross-stitch design fits and is arranged as desired on a particular pattern, it is a good idea to first chart the design.

To do this, make an enlarged photocopy of the gridded pattern (to make it easier to color in the squares) from a project in this book (we have given permission for making copies of the patterns for personal use on *page 2*) or copy the pattern outline onto graph paper. Because the patterns given are all full-size, the original pattern will give you a good idea of how big your finished project will be.

To chart your design, you will need the following supplies: graph paper or a photocopied pattern from this book, colored pencils, a ruler, and a sharp pencil or fine-tipped marking pen.

On the copy of the pattern, carefully copy the selected chart(s) using pencil colors similar to those used on the original chart (see *above*). If you want to repeat the symbols, use a fine-tipped marking pen (an enlargement of the pattern would be helpful if you wish to do this). If you want a design centered on a pattern, match the center of the design with the center of the pattern

■ *Once a pattern from this book is photocopied, simply copy desired designs using colored pencils. If adding symbols from the color key, make the photocopy an enlargement before coloring in the grid.*

(see how we centered the word "Joy" left to right).

If you wish to repeat a pattern, be sure to leave the same number of squares between the charted motifs (remember, on our charted design, one box of graph paper is equal to two threads on 28-count fabric).

from start to finish

charting letters and numbers

The best way to be certain a name, word, or series of words or numbers accurately fits a design is to chart it before beginning to stitch. Simply copy the chosen letters or numbers onto graph paper, leaving a equal number of spaces (threads) between letters or digits.

converting designs to other count fabrics

As we mentioned, all designs in this book are stitched over two threads on 28-count fabric. To determine the finished size of any cross-stitch design, first record the stitch count of the design. Then record the stitch count of the fabric. If stitching over two threads, divide this number in half. This will give you the number of cross-stitches per inch (see *below*). Here is an easy way to determine the finished stitched sizes:
Example: The "Joy" design measures 35wx15h. If the design is stitched over two threads of 28 count fabric.
35 ÷ 14= 2½
15 ÷ 14 = 1¹⁄₁₆
Stitched over two threads of 28-count fabric, the "Joy" design will measure 2½ inches wide by 1¹⁄₁₆ inches high.

What if you would like to stitch a certain design for a button cover, but the stitch count is too big for 14-squares-per-inch fabric? You can simply change your fabric choice to a more-squares-per-inch fabric or try stitching over one thread instead of two.

See the chart, *below right*, to see how the finished size for the 35w×15h "Joy" design changes when stitched over two threads of a variety of fabrics:

stitching on perforated plastic, plastic canvas, and perforated paper

When you prefer to stitch on a material other than cross-stitch fabric, you can substitute cross-stitch plastics or perforated papers, calculating your finished design size to meet your needs. These stitching materials do not allow for fractional stitches, so you may want to redesign motifs that are charted using fractional stitches. To finish the edge, simply trim one square beyond the stitching on all sides. A whipstitch is often used to finish the edges on plastic canvas.

changing floss colors

If you would like to change the colors of a particular cross-stitch design, it is a good idea to select a new color for each floss number listed in the color key. To do this it is much easier if you have a floss book on hand that provides samples of each floss color. When changing a red rose to a

---

Stitch count width ÷ fabric count = width of stitched design
Stitch count height ÷ fabric count = height of stitched design

---

14-count (7-count)—5×2⅛
18-count (9-count)—3⁷⁄₈×1⅝
20-count (10-count)—3½×1½
25-count (12.5-count)—2⁷⁄₈×1¼
28-count (14-count)—2½×1¹⁄₁₆
32-count (16-count)—2⅛×⁷⁄₈
45-count (22.5-count)—1⅝×⅝

pink one, for example, try selecting pink tones that are similar in intensity to the red flosses given.

It is wise to chart your new design using colored pencils similar to the colors of floss you have chosen. If you like what you see, begin stitching. If you wish to make changes, now is the time.

The color wheel, *below*, can help you understand why some colors work well together while others seem to clash. Colors that are adjacent to one another on the wheel will blend quietly. To enliven a color, add one from the opposite side. All colors alter in appearance when placed next to different colors.

blending floss

What if you need a medium tone of red/orange but you used the last ply on your last project? Blending other floss colors may achieve the color you want. Try using one ply of a light red/orange with one ply of a dark red/orange. If this produces a color similar to the medium tone you want, simply stitch with the blended floss plies.

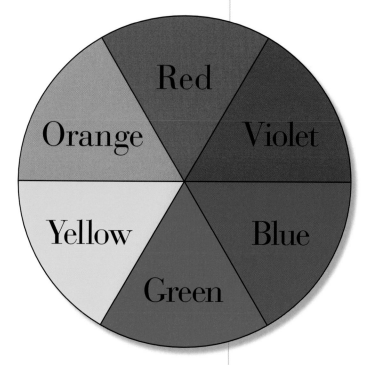

C ompiled for your easy reference, in alphabetical order, we've collected 48 of the most often used specialty stitches on the following pages. Combine these beautiful stitches with your favorite motifs from this book to design your own samplers, or use them to add special details or borders to your cross-stitched works of art.

specialty stitches

specialty stitches

Here they are—all of the specialty stitches that you will need to complete any of the designs in this book! Plus, we've included many more stitch diagrams that you may want at your fingertips for easy reference. Each stitch is beautifully illustrated and groups of illustrations for one stitch are boxed for your convenience. We have labeled each diagram with the most common name for that stitch.

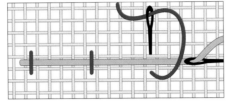

Couching Stitch

Diagonal Satin Stitch

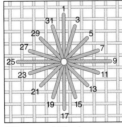

Diamond Eyelet

Double
Leviathan Stitch

Algerian Eyelet

Blanket Stitch

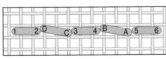

Double Running Stitch

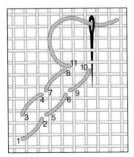

Cable Stitch

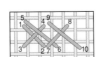

Doubleback Stitch

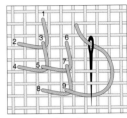

Elongated Star Stitch

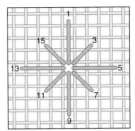

Feather Stitch

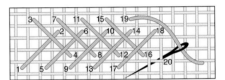

Fishbone

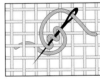

Four-Sided
Backstitch

French Knot

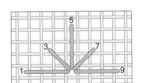

Half Diamond Eyelet

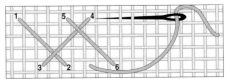

Herringbone Stitch

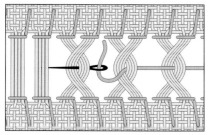

Inverted Warps

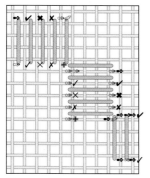

Kloster Block

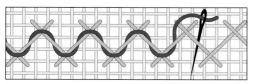

Laced Herringbone

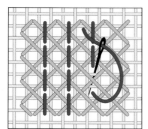

Laid Work with Couching

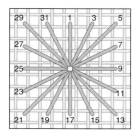

Large Algerian Eyelet

Lazy Daisy

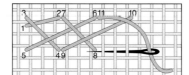

Long Arm Cross-Stitch

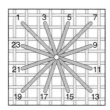

Medium Algerian Eyelet

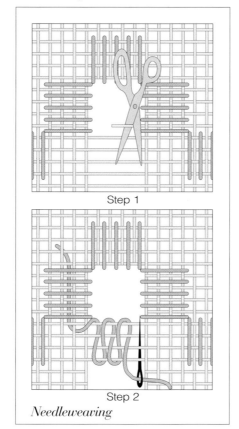

Needleweaving

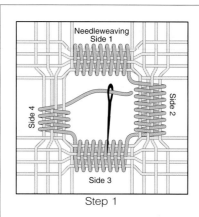

Needleweaving with Dove's Eye

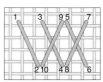

Oblong Stitch

specialty stitches

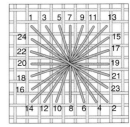

Rhodes Stitch

Rice Stitch

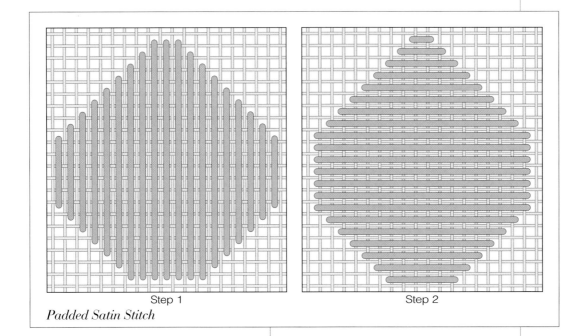

Step 1

Step 2

Padded Satin Stitch

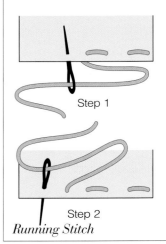

Step 1

Step 2

Running Stitch

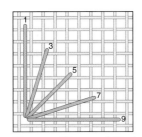

Quarter Diamond Eyelet

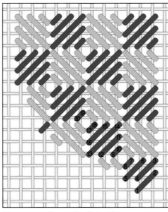

Reverse Scotch Stitch

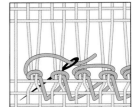

Satin Stitch

Serpentine Stitch

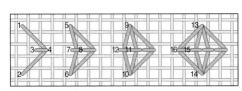

Queen Stitch

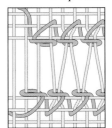

Serpentine Stitch Variation

Small Algerian
Eyelet

Smyrna
Cross-Stitch

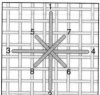

Star Stitch

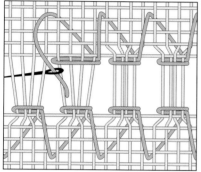

Straight Hemstitch

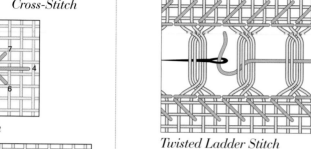

Twisted Ladder Stitch

Upright
Cross-Stitch

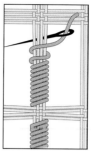

Wrapped Bars

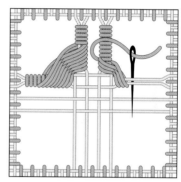

Wrapped Bars with
Adjoining Wrap

Tent Stitch

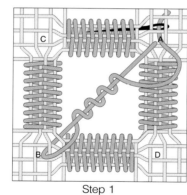

Step 1

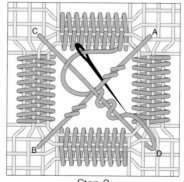

Step 2

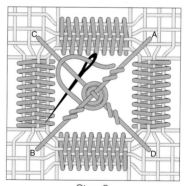

Step 3

Woven Wheel and Spokes

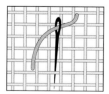 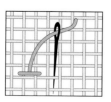 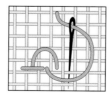 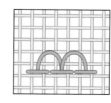 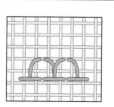

Turkey Work

In this chapter of patterns and instructions you'll get ideas and full-sized patterns on graphs for making a variety of projects using the motifs in this book. The stitching instructions for each design can be found opposite the original charts. Turn the page for inspiring projects you can make with confidence. Refer to *pages 300–305* for tips on designing so you can personalize these projects with your own flair and creative style.

patterns & instructions

patterns & instructions

■ fabric and floss

For each button cover:
5x5-inch piece of 28-count cross-stitch fabric in desired color
5x5-inch piece of lightweight fusible interfacing
Cotton embroidery floss listed in key of chosen design

■ supplies

For each button cover:
Needle; 1½-inch button cover form
Sewing thread; wire cutters
¾-inch-diameter button cover finding
All-purpose cement

■ instructions

Trace or copy the outline of the pattern, *above right,* onto 14-count graph paper or photocopy the pattern. Chart desired motif onto the graph making sure no designs extend beyond the design area indicated by the dashed line. *Note: The solid outline on this pattern indicates the gathering line, the cutting line is ¼ inch beyond this line.*

Zigzag-stitch or overcast the edges of the fabric to prevent fraying. Find the center of the chart and of the fabric; begin stitching there over two threads.

Fuse the interfacing to the back of the stitched fabric following the manufacturer's instructions. Center the fabric over the button-cover form and trim to ½ inch beyond the edge of the form. Run a gathering thread ¼ inch from the cut edge. Pull up the gathering thread to smooth the fabric. Assemble the button cover following the manufacturer's instructions. Remove the button shank using the wire cutters. Glue the button cover to the finding using all-purpose cement.

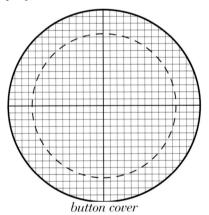

button cover

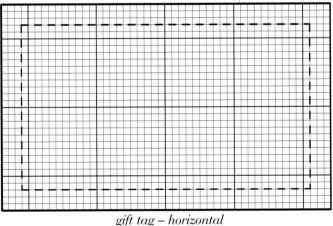

gift tag – horizontal

■ fabric and floss

4x5-inch piece of 14-count perforated paper in desired color
Cotton embroidery floss listed in key of chosen design

■ supplies

Needle; #5 pearl cotton in desired color for edging

■ instructions

Trace or copy the outline of the pattern, *below left,* onto 14-count graph paper or photocopy the pattern. Chart desired motif onto the graph, keeping the design at least three squares from the edges.

Find the center of the chart and of the perforated paper; begin stitching there. Using the pattern, *left,* trim the tag to the finished size.

Use one strand of pearl cotton to work blanket stitches *(see page 308)* around the edges of the perforated paper. Stitch through every other hole skipping two holes, if needed, when coming to a corner so the stitch falls in the corner. Work a second stitch at each corner. Continue working blanket stitches until all sides are completed.

mantel scarf

Use this pattern to create a mantel scarf for any holiday or season.

Design Choices: All-over repeat patterns, Christmas or holiday border patterns, or Christmas motifs will work for this project.

fabric and floss

Seven 6x7-inch pieces of 28-count cross-stitch fabric in desired color
1 yard of 45-inch-wide plaid fabric
1 yard of 45-inch-wide muslin fabric
Cotton embroidery floss listed in key of chosen design

supplies

Needle; embroidery hoop
Sewing thread to match fabrics
Seven 2-inch-long tassels in desired color
Eight ½-inch-diameter gold jingle bells, optional

instructions

Trace or copy the outline of the pattern, *above right*, onto 14-count graph paper or photocopy the pattern. Chart desired motifs onto the graph making sure the design *does not* extend beyond the dashed stitching lines. (You can chart seven different designs for the stitched tabs, stitch the same design, or alternate designs.)

Zigzag-stitch or serge the edges of the cross-stitch fabric. Find the center of one chart and the center of one piece of cross-stitch fabric; begin stitching there over two threads. Repeat for the remaining mantel tabs.

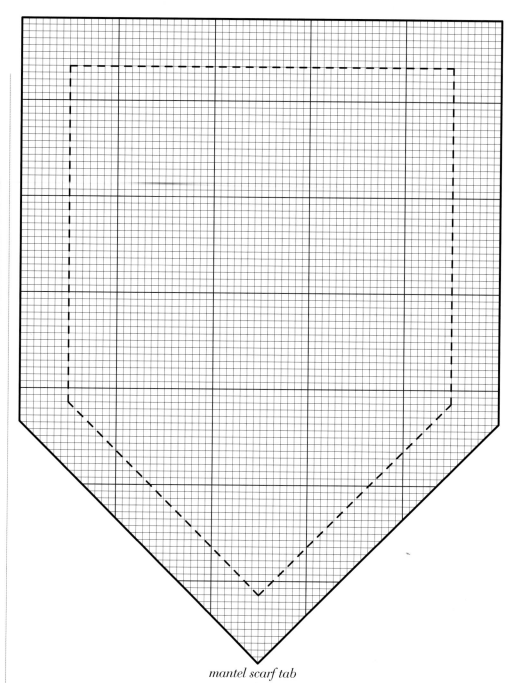

mantel scarf tab

Use the pattern to cut seven shapes from the plaid fabric. All measurements include a ½-inch seam allowance. With right sides together, sew the plaid fabric to the stitched tab, leaving the top open for turning. Clip the corners, turn, and press. Set aside.

Cut a 9×41-inch piece each from the plaid fabric and from the muslin. With

right sides facing, sew one long side and the two ends together. Clip the corners, turn, and press.

Turn under ½ inch along the open side. Insert the raw edges of the stitched tabs within the fold of the long strip, with one tab at each end and then spacing the remaining tabs 2 inches apart. Topstitch the tabs in place.

patterns & instructions

■ fabric and floss

10x5½-inch piece of 28-count
 cross-stitch fabric in desired color
Cotton embroidery floss listed in key
 of chosen design

■ supplies

Needle; sewing thread to match fabric
Two 7-inch-long pieces of ⅛-inch-wide
 satin ribbon in desired color

■ instructions

Trace or copy the outline of the pattern, *right*, onto 14-count graph paper or photocopy the pattern. The fold will be the bottom of the bag. Chart desired motifs onto the graph, making sure the design *does not* extend beyond the dashed stitching lines.

 Fold the cross-stitch fabric in half to measure 5½x5 inches. Find center of chart and center of one half of cross-stitch fabric; begin stitching there over two threads.

 Sew bag side seams, right sides together, with raw edges even. The pattern and all the measurements include a ½-inch seam allowance. Trim seams and turn. Press under ½ inch along opening; tack in place.

 For handle, sew ends of ribbons to insides of each bag.

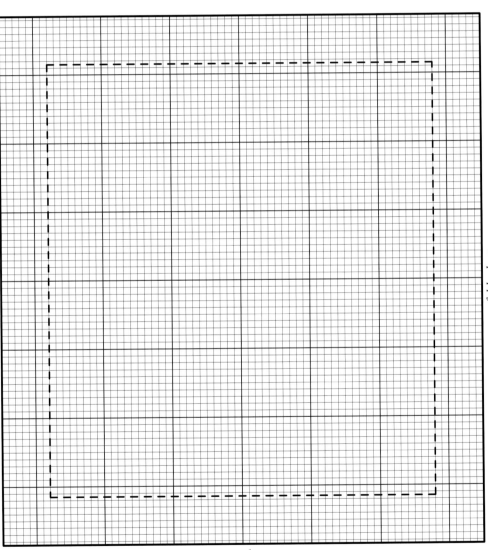

fold—bottom

treat bag

stacking blocks

Use this pattern to create stacking blocks for a country decorating accent.

Design Choices: Alphabet letters with no fractional stitches will work for this project.

fabric and floss

Six 3x3-inch pieces of 14-count brown perforated paper

Cotton embroidery floss as listed in key of chosen design

supplies

Needle
2½-inch wooden blocks
Acrylic paints in desired colors
Paintbrush
Assorted buttons
Crafts glue
Wood glue

instructions

Trace or copy the outline of the pattern six times, *below left*, onto 14-count graph paper or photocopy the pattern. Chart desired motifs onto the graphs, making sure the designs keep at least one square within the dashed lines.

For each side of the block, find the center of the chart and the center of the perforated paper; begin stitching there.

Trim the stitched paper to measure 2×2 inches, as indicated by the outline on the pattern. *Note: This will allow the paint to show and room to attach buttons.*

Paint the wooden blocks using acrylic paint as desired. Allow to dry. Glue each stitched piece to a side of the wood block; glue buttons to the corners of the paper.

brooch

Use this pattern to create a brooch with a single bloom, initials, or other small motif.

Design Choices: All-over repeat patterns, border patterns, or small motifs will work for this project

fabric and floss

6x6-inch piece 28-count cross-stitch fabric in desired color

4x4-inch piece of lightweight fusible interfacing

Cotton embroidery floss listed in key of chosen design

supplies

Needle
Embroidery hoop
1⅞-inch button form
Pin back
All-purpose cement

instructions

Trace or copy the outline of the pattern, *below*, onto 14-count graph paper or simply photocopy the pattern. Chart desired motif onto the graph, making sure no designs extend beyond the dashed line.

Tape or zigzag edges of fabric to prevent fraying. Find center of the chart and the center of the fabric; begin stitching there over two threads.

Fuse interfacing to back of the linen following manufacturer's instructions. Center design over button form; trim fabric ½ inch beyond edge. Run a gathering thread ¼ inch from cut edge; tighten gathers. Assemble button following the manufacturer's instructions.

Remove the button shank. Cement the pin back to the back of the button form.

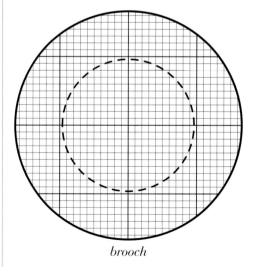

brooch

block

patterns & instructions

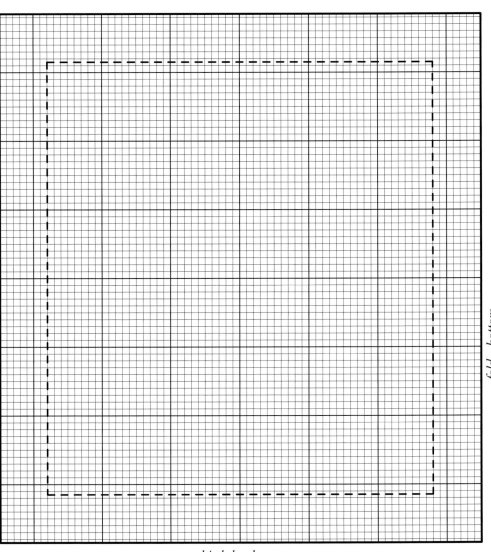

birthday bag

birthday bag

Use this pattern to create birthday bags to hold tiny surprises.

Design Choices: All-over repeat patterns, border patterns, or small motifs will work for this project. We suggest using the Flowers of the Month motifs.

▪ fabric and floss

10x5½-inch piece of 28-count
   cross-stitch fabric in desired color
9x5-inch piece of fabric for lining
Cotton embroidery floss as listed in
   key of chosen design

▪ supplies

Needle; embroidery hoop
9-inch piece of ¾-inch-wide flat lace
10-inch piece of ¼-inch wide
   picot-edged satin ribbon

▪ instructions

Trace or copy the outline of the pattern, *right,* onto 14-count graph paper or photocopy the pattern. Chart desired motifs onto the graph, making sure no designs extend beyond the dashed lines. The pattern includes ½-inch seam allowances. Pieces are sewn with right sides facing unless otherwise specified.

  Fold the cross-stitch fabric in half to measure 5½x5 inches. Find the vertical center of the chart and of one half of cross-stitch fabric; begin stitching there over two threads.

  Fold the cross-stitch fabric, right sides together, with the edges even. Sew the side seams; *do not* turn. Sew the lining together in the same manner. Trim all of the seams. Tuck the stitched piece of fabric into the lining and stitch the top edge together. Trim the seam; turn.

  Baste the lace around the top of the bag. Slip-stitch the ends of the ribbon to the inside top at the sides of the bag.

  Fill the birthday bag with wrapped candies, a small gift, or a gift certificate.

fold—bottom

diamond ornament

Use this pattern to create ornaments for Christmas and Easter.

Design Choices: All-over repeat patterns, border patterns, or small motifs will work for this project.

fabric and floss

6x6-inch piece of 28-count cross-stitch fabric in desired color

5x5-inch piece of white felt

Cotton embroidery floss listed in key of chosen design

supplies

Needle

Embroidery hoop

Tracing paper

Erasable fabric marker

Crafts glue

5x5-inch piece of self-stick mounting board with foam

12-inch piece of ¼-inch-wide rattail cord

12-inch piece of ½-inch trim

5-inch piece of ⅛-inch-diameter metallic cord

Purchased 3-inch-long tassel

Two purchased 2-inch-long tassels

instructions

Trace or copy the outline of the pattern, *right*, onto 14-count graph paper or photocopy the pattern. Chart desired motifs onto the graph, making sure the design does not extend beyond the dashed lines.

Tape or zigzag edges of fabric to prevent fraying. Find the center of the chart and the center of the fabric; begin stitching there over two threads.

Trace the ornament outline from the pattern onto tracing paper; cut out. Center the pattern over the stitched piece.

Use erasable marker to the trace around the pattern; *do not* cut out. Use the tracing paper pattern to cut one shape each from the mounting board and from the felt.

Peel the protective paper from the mounting board. Center the foam side on the back of the stitchery and press to stick. Trim excess fabric ½ inch beyond edges of board. Fold raw edges of fabric to back and glue.

Glue the rattail cord around the front of the ornament. Glue the cord behind rattail. Glue the rim behind the cord.

Fold the remaining piece of ⅛-inch cord in half and glue the ends of the cord to the top point of the ornament for a hanger. Glue the large tassel to the opposite point of ornament. Glue the small tassels to the side points. Glue felt to the back of the ornament.

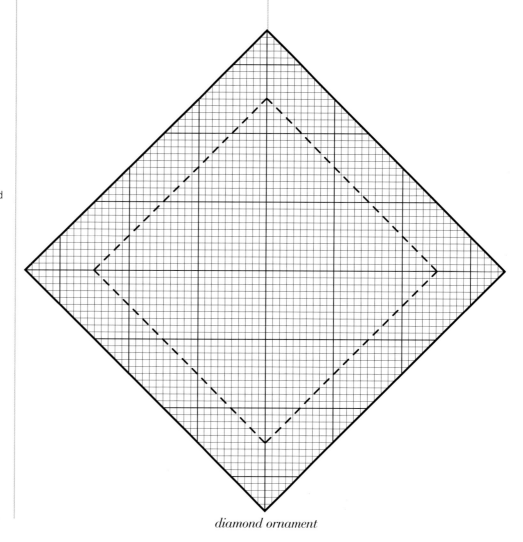

diamond ornament

patterns & instructions

heart ornament

Use this pattern to create ornaments for Valentine's Day, Christmas, and more.

Design Choices: All-over repeat patterns, border patterns, or small motifs will work for this project.

▪ fabric and floss

6x6-inch piece of 28-count cross-stitch
    fabric in desired color
4x4-inch piece of felt in desired color
Cotton embroidery floss listed in key
    of chosen design

▪ supplies

Needle; embroidery hoop; tracing paper
Erasable fabric marker; crafts glue
5x5-inch piece of self-stick
    mounting board with foam;
    14-inch piece of
    ¼-inch-wide braid
14-inch piece of
    ¼-inch-diameter cording
Two 5-inch pieces of
    ⅛-inch-diameter cording

▪ instructions

Trace or copy outline of pattern, *right*, onto 14-count graph paper or photocopy the pattern. Chart desired motifs onto the graph, making sure the designs *do not* extend beyond the dashed line.

Tape or zigzag edges of cross-stitch fabric. Find the center of chart and of fabric; begin stitching there over two threads.

Trace the ornament outline from the pattern onto tracing paper; cut out. Center the pattern over the stitched piece. Use erasable marker to trace around the pattern; *do not* cut out. Use tracing paper pattern to cut one shape each from mounting board and felt.

Peel protective paper from mounting board. Center the foam side on back of stitchery and press to stick. Trim excess fabric ½ inch beyond edges of board. Fold raw edges of fabric to back and glue.

Glue braid around edge of the heart. Glue wide cording behind the braid. Tie one piece of narrow cord into a bow; glue to the top center of the heart. Fold remaining piece of cord in half; glue the ends to the top center of the ornament. Glue felt to the back.

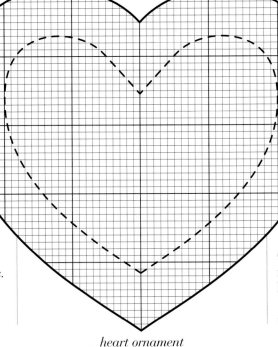

heart ornament

belt buckle

Use this pattern to stitch a belt buckle that covers a perforated plastic form.

Design Choices: All-over repeat patterns, border patterns, or small motifs will work for this project.

▪ fabric and floss

6x6-inch piece of 28-count cross-stitch
    fabric in desired color
5x5-inch piece of lightweight
    iron-on interfacing
5x5-inch piece of polyester fleece
5x5-inch piece of felt
Cotton embroidery floss listed in key
    of chosen design

▪ supplies

Needle; embroidery hoop
Erasable marker
Tracing paper
8x5-inch piece of
    perforated plastic
1-inch-wide silver belting to
    fit waist measurement
Purchased belt buckle
Crafts glue

▪ instructions

Trace or copy the outline of the pattern, *page 321*, onto 14-count graph paper or photocopy the pattern. Chart desired motifs onto the graph, making sure the designs *do not* extend beyond the dashed line.

Tape or zigzag the edges of the fabric to prevent fraying. Find the center of the chart and center of the fabric; begin stitching there over two threads.

Place tracing paper over the pattern and trace the oval outline; cut out. Center the stitchery under the pattern and cut out. Place the tracing paper over the pattern again and trace the dashed-line oval. Use this pattern to cut two shapes from perforated plastic and one from felt. Fuse interfacing to the back of cross-stitch fabric following the manufacturer's instructions. Trim to fit stitchery size. Use stitched piece as a pattern to cut one more from fleece.

Baste plastic ovals together. Glue fleece to plastic. Fold excess fleece to back and glue. Center stitchery over fleece-covered shape. Run a gathering thread ¼ inch from cut edge; pull gathers to smooth. Glue edges to back. Glue felt to back.

Assemble belt following manufacturer's instructions. Whipstitch finished oval to the belt buckle.

miniature stockings

Use this pattern to create miniature stocking ornaments made from perforated paper

Design Choices: All-over repeat patterns, borders, or any small Christmas motif without fractional stitches will work for this project.

fabric and floss

For each stocking
5x4-inch piece of 14-count
    perforated paper
Cotton embroidery floss listed in key
    of chosen design

supplies

Needle; pencil
    17-inch piece of rattail cord

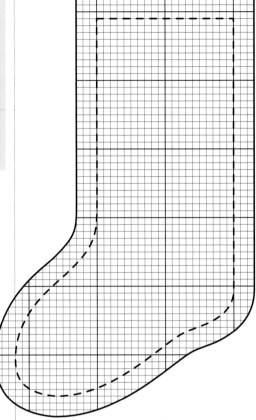

miniature stocking

instructions

Trace or copy the outline of the pattern, *above*, onto 14-count graph paper or photocopy the pattern. Chart desired motifs onto the graph, making sure the designs *do not* extend beyond the dashed line. Cut the pattern out around the outline.

Find the center of the chart and the center of the perforated paper; begin stitching there.

Center the pattern over the stitched piece; trace around the pattern and cut out the stocking.

Glue cord around the edge of the stocking, starting at the top right corner. Fold the excess cord into a loop and glue to the back of the stocking.

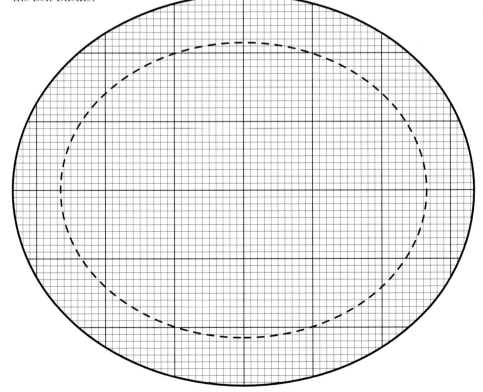

belt buckle

patterns & instructions

fabric and floss

7x5-inch piece of 28-count cross-stitch fabric in desired color

7x5½-inch piece of lightweight fusible interfacing

7x5½-inch piece of white broadcloth

Cotton embroidery floss listed in key of chosen design

supplies

Tracing paper; erasable marker

Needle; embroidery hoop

4½-inch-long piece of 1¹⁄₁₆-inch-diameter wooden dowel

⅔ yard of ⅛-inch-diameter twisted satin cord

2-inch-long purchased tassel

Sewing thread; crafts glue

instructions

Trace or copy the outline of the pattern, *right*, onto 14-count graph paper or photocopy the pattern. Chart desired motifs onto the graph, making sure the designs *do not* extend beyond the dashed lines.

Tape or zigzag the edges of the cross-stitch fabric to prevent fraying. Center and stitch the desired motif over two threads.

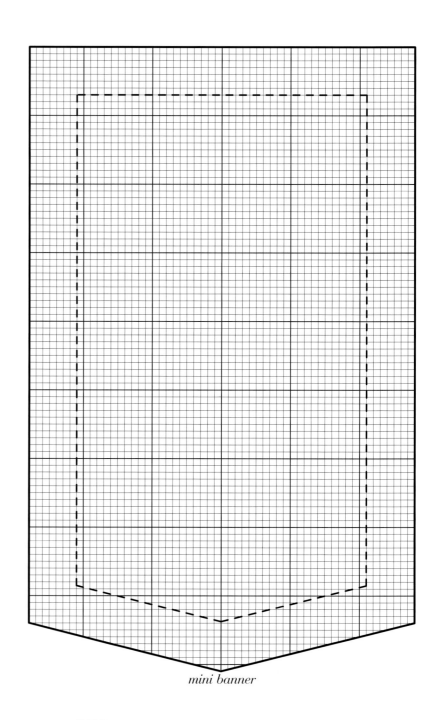

mini banner

Fuse the interfacing to the back of the fabric. Using tracing paper, trace around the pattern; cut out. Draw around the pattern on the stitched piece; cut out. Use the stitchery as a pattern to cut a matching back from the broadcloth.

Sew the two pieces together, right sides together, using ½-inch seams and leaving the top edge open. Clip the corners, turn right side out, and press. Slip-stitch the opening closed.

Cut a 14½-inch piece of cord. Apply glue to the cord ends to prevent fraying. Slip-stitch the cord to the side and bottom edges of the ornament. For casing, fold 1 inch of the top edge to the back; slip-stitch. Insert the dowel. Tie the ends of the remaining cord to the dowel ends, leaving 1-inch tails. Tack the cord in place and fringe the tails. Tack the tassel to the bottom center of the ornament.

jar topper
Use this pattern to create jar toppers for homemade canned goods to give with love.

Design Choices: All-over repeat patterns, borders, or any small holiday motif will work for this project.

▓ fabric and floss
- 6x6-inch piece of 28-count cross-stitch fabric in desired color
- ⅓ yard of 45-inch-wide calico fabric
- 5-inch-diameter circle of lightweight fusible interfacing
- Cotton embroidery floss listed in key of chosen design

▓ supplies
- Needle; embroidery hoop
- Sewing thread
- 10-inch piece of ⅙-inch-diameter elastic cord
- 20-inch piece of ¼-inch-wide satin ribbon

▓ instructions
Trace or copy the outline of the pattern, *below*, onto 14-count graph paper or photocopy the pattern. Chart desired motifs onto the graph, making sure the designs *do not* extend beyond the dashed line.

Tape or zigzag the edges of fabric to prevent fraying. Find the center of chart and of the fabric; begin stitching there over two threads.

Fuse interfacing to the back of the cross-stitch fabric following the manufacturer's instructions. Centering the design, cut the stitched fabric into a 4-inch-diameter circle as indicated by the heavy line on the pattern.

From the calico fabric, cut a 37×3⅛-inch bias strip. With the right sides together, sew the short ends of the strip to form a continuous circle.

Sew a ⅛-inch hem in one long edge of the strip. Run gathering threads ⅜ inch and ¼ inch from the other long edge of the strip. On wrong side of fabric, machine zigzag stitch over the elastic cord 1 inch from the hemmed edge.

Gather the ruffle to fit the perimeter of the cross-stitch fabric circle. With the right sides together, baste the ruffle to the fabric. Adjust the gathers and stitch using a ¼-inch seam allowance. Tighten elastic to fit jar. Secure the free end of the elastic. Slip topper over jar. Tie ribbon around topper; knot ribbon ends.

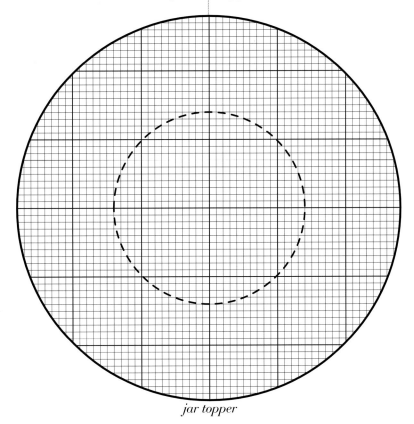

jar topper

patterns & instructions

mitten ornaments

Use this pattern to create miniature mittens to hang on a tree, banister, or mantel.

Design Choices: All-over repeat patterns, borders, or any small Christmas motif will work for this project.

fabric and floss

6x6-inch piece of 28-count cross-stitch
    fabric in desired color
3½x3-inch piece *each* of fleece and felt
Cotton embroidery floss listed in key
    of chosen design

supplies

Needle; embroidery hoop
½ yard of ⅛-inch-diameter cord

instructions

Trace or copy the outline of the pattern, *right*, onto 14-count graph paper or photocopy the pattern. Chart desired motifs onto the graph, making sure the designs *do not* extend beyond the dashed line. Cut out the pattern.

Tape or zigzag the edges of the cross-stitch fabric to prevent fraying. Find the center of a chart and of the fabric; begin stitching there over two threads.

Center the pattern over the stitchery and trace. Use the pattern to cut a mitten shape from fleece and from felt for the mitten back. Baste the fleece to the back of the stitched piece, ¼ inch from the edge.

Sew the front to the felt back along the basting lines, right sides together, leaving the top open. Clip the curves; turn. Fold the top edge over the fleece; baste to felt. Tack the cord around the mitten edge, except for the top. Tie the cord ends in a bow for a hanger; knot ends of cord.

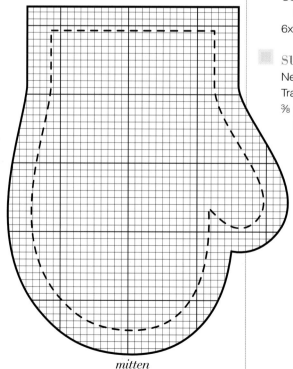

mitten

ornament

Use this pattern to create arch-shaped holiday ornaments.

Design Choices: All-over repeat patterns, borders, or any small motif will work for this project.

fabric and floss

6x7-inch piece of 28-count cross-stitch
    fabric in desired color
¼ yard 45-inch-wide fabric in
    desired color
6x7-inch piece polyester fleece
Cotton embroidery floss listed in key
    of chosen design
6x7-inch piece of felt

supplies

Needle; embroidery hoop
Tracing paper
⅜ yard of ⅛-inch-diameter cotton cord
    6x7-inch piece *each* medium and
        lightweight cardboard
    Crafts glue

instructions

Trace or copy the outline of the pattern onto 14-count graph paper or photocopy the pattern. Chart desired motifs onto the graph, making sure designs do not extend beyond dashed line.

Tape or zigzag edges of fabric to prevent fraying. Find center of chart and fabric; begin stitching there over two threads.

Using the tracing paper, trace the pattern and cut out. Draw around tracing paper pattern on cross-stitched fabric; cut out. Using the dashed lines as a pattern, trace this pattern and cut one each of fleece, cardboard, and felt. Cut out each along lines.

Glue fleece to medium-weight cardboard. Center cross-stitch fabric, right side up, over fleece; fold edges to back and glue. Center the fabric arch shape over the lightweight cardboard and glue. Glue the felt to the back.

Glue twisted cord around the edge of the ornament. Add a loop at the top for a hanger.

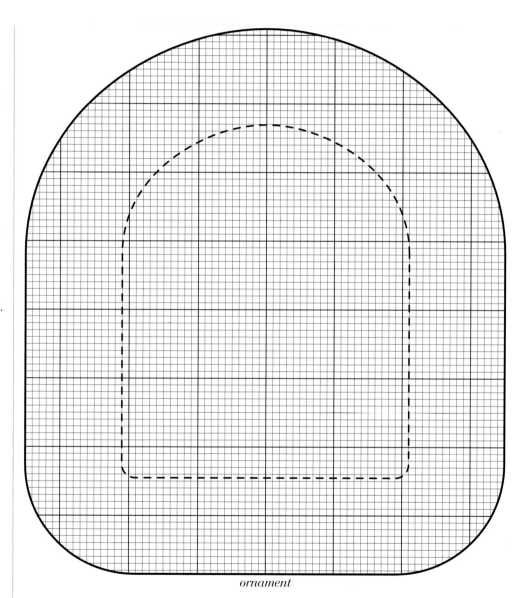

ornament

patterns & instructions

key chain

Use this pattern to create personalized key chains.

Design Choices: All-over repeat patterns, borders, or small motifs without fractional stitches will work for this project.

fabric and floss

- 2x6-inch piece of 14-count perforated plastic
- Two 3x6-inch pieces of imitation suede fabric in two desired colors
- Cotton embroidery floss listed in key of chosen design

supplies

- Needle
- Tacky fabric glue
- Pinking shears
- Key chain finding with jump ring

instructions

Trace or copy the outline of the pattern, *below*, onto 14-count graph paper or photocopy the pattern. Chart desired motifs onto the graph, making sure design leaves at least one square unstitched around the edge. Cut out the pattern.

Find the center of the chart and the center of the perforated plastic; begin stitching there.

Center the pattern over the stitched piece of plastic, trace around pattern; trim if needed. Glue the stitched piece to one piece of the imitation suede fabric. Using pinking shears, trim the suede ⅛ inch beyond the plastic. Glue the piece to the second piece of suede fabric. Trim to ⅛ inch beyond the first piece of suede fabric along the top, bottom, and left side edges. On right side edge, cut a point ending ¾ inch beyond the stitched plastic.

Attach the jump ring of the key chain finding to the pointed end of the fabric, ¼ inch from the tip.

large holiday heart ornament

Use this pattern to create festive holiday ornaments or sweet sachets filled with potpourri.

Design Choices: All-over larger repeat pattern, borders, or any floral motif will work for this project.

fabric and floss

- 11x11-inch piece of 28-count cross-stitch fabric in desired color
- 6x6-inch piece of felt
- 6x6-inch piece of fleece
- Cotton embroidery floss listed in key of chosen design

supplies

- Needle; embroidery hoop; tracing paper
- 6x6-inch piece of medium-weight cardboard
- Crafts glue
- ⅞ yard of twisted satin cord
- ⅝ yard of ½-inch-wide flat lace
- 3-inch tassel to match satin cord

instructions

Trace or copy the outline of the pattern, *opposite*, onto 14-count graph paper or photocopy the pattern. Chart desired motifs onto the graph, making sure the design *does not* extend beyond the dashed line.

Tape or zigzag edges of fabric to prevent fraying. Find the center of the chart and of the fabric; begin stitching there over two threads.

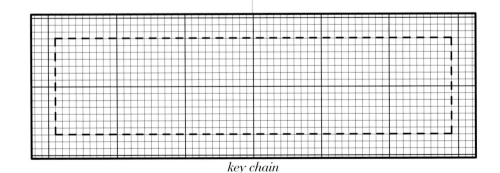

key chain

Using tracing paper, trace the heart pattern and cut out on dashed lines. Use this pattern to cut one heart each from cardboard, fleece, and felt. Center and pin the pattern onto the stitched fabric; cut out ½ inch beyond edge of pattern.

Glue the fleece heart to the cardboard. Center the stitched fabric over the fleece-covered cardboard. Fold excess cross-stitch fabric to the back and glue.

Cut enough cord to fit around edge of heart; glue, overlapping ends on back.

Position and glue lace behind cord. Fold remaining cord in half and knot about 1 inch below fold. Glue ends of cord to top center of heart back. Glue tassel to bottom of heart back. Position and glue felt to back.

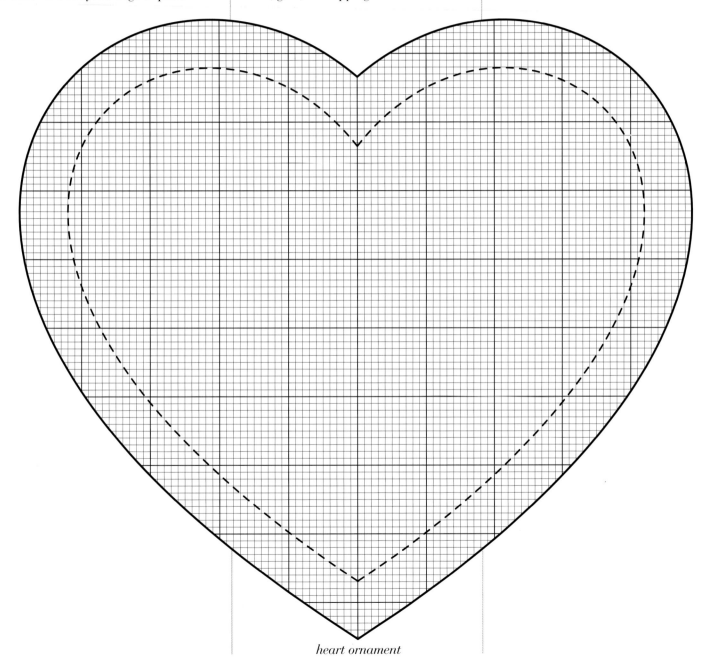

heart ornament

patterns & instructions

fabric and floss

- 7x7-inch piece of 28-count cross-stitch fabric in desired color
- Cotton embroidery floss listed in key of chosen design

supplies

- Needle
- Embroidery hoop
- Small hand mirror with mounting board and a 3½-inch-diameter opening for inserting cross-stitch (see Sources, *page 335*)
- White fabric marker
- Thread to match cross-stitch fabric
- 12 inches of ⅜-inch-wide flat braid
- 4x4-inch piece of batting
- Fabric glue
- Crafts glue

instructions

Trace or copy the outline of the pattern, *right*, onto 14-count graph paper or photocopy the pattern. Chart desired motifs onto the graph, making sure design *does not* extend beyond dashed line.

Tape or zigzag the edges of the cross-stitch fabric. Find the center of the chart, and the center of the fabric; begin stitching there over two threads.

Centering the mounting board over the design, draw a circle around the stitchery, ¼ inch larger than the mounting board. Use doubled thread to run gathering stitches around marked circle. Leave a ¾-inch tail and knot thread.

Cut batting slightly smaller than mounting board; center on the top of the board.

Steam back of stitchery to soften. Pull opposite corners to straighten as necessary. While the fabric is damp, position the batting-covered board on back of stitchery and pull the thread tight, gathering to fit.

Trim excess fabric to within ¼ inch of stitching. Allow stitchery to dry completely on mounting board.

Glue braid around perimeter of covered board; allow glue to dry.

Glue the board into the recess in the mirror. Weight down until the glue dries.

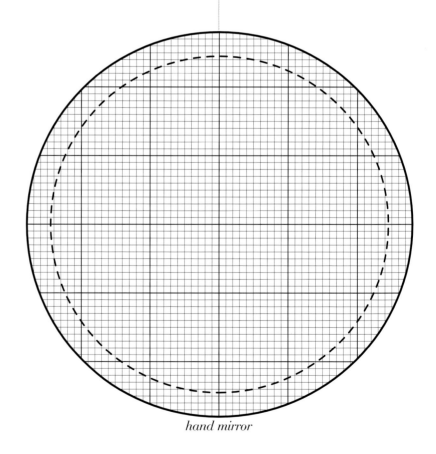

hand mirror

plant poke

Use this pattern to create plant pokes to personalize a gift from nature.

Design Choices: All-over repeat patterns, borders, or small motifs without fractional stitches will work for this project.

fabric and floss

For one plant poke

3x4-inch piece of 14-count
  perforated plastic
Two 3x5-inch pieces of imitation suede
  fabric in desired colors
Cotton embroidery floss listed in key
  of chosen design

supplies

Needle
½x¼x18-inch strip of balsa wood
Crafts glue; pinking shears
Acrylic paint in two colors as desired
Paintbrush; acrylic spray varnish
Two 1-yard lengths of ⅛- or ¼-inch-wide
  ribbon in desired colors

instructions

Trace or copy the outline of the pattern, *below*, onto 14-count graph paper or photocopy the pattern. Chart desired motifs onto the graph, making sure design leaves at least one square unstitched around the edge. Cut out the pattern.

Find the center of the chart and the center of the plastic; begin stitching there.

Center pattern over stitchery and trace. Cut out plastic. Center plastic on one piece of imitation suede fabric; glue. Cut fabric ¼ inch beyond plastic using pinking shears. Next, glue to second piece of imitation suede fabric. Cut the fabric ¼ inch beyond first fabric using pinking shears.

To decorate the balsa wood stake, paint the wood a solid color. To make polka-dots with a second color, simply dip the end of a paintbrush into paint and dab it on the surface of the stake. When dry, spray with varnish.

Glue the fabric-backed cross-stitch design to the wood stake near the top. Tie ribbons into a bow around the stake at base of the stitched design.

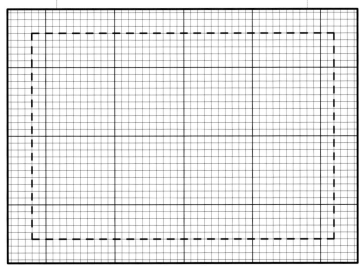

plant poke

index

index

index

sources & credits

fabrics

Zweigart, 2 Riverview Dr., Somerset, NJ 08873-1139, 908/271-1949.

threads

Anchor, Consumer Service Dept., P.O. Box 27067, Greenville, SC 29616; DMC, Port Kearney Building 10, South Kearney, NJ 07032-0650.

supplies

Hand Mirror, *page 328*, Sudberry House, Old Lyme, CT 06371.

mounting

Dot's Frame Shop, 4223 Fleur Drive, Des Moines, IA 50321; Walnut Street Gallery, 301 SW Walnut Street, Ankeny, IA 50021.

photography

Plate and floss photography by Andy Lyons Cameraworks. Image photography by Adobe Systems Inc.: *pages 4, 5, 44, 46, 52, 54, 68, 70, 72, 82, 84, 104, 106, 242, 244, 246, 248, 250, 252, 254, 256, 258, 260, 262, 264, 266, 268, 270, 272, 274, 276, and 278.* Artville: *pages 126, 140, 142, 160, 162, and 164.* Paul Avis/Tony Stone Images: *pages 280, 290, and 292.* Lori Adamski Peek / Tony Stone Images: *pages 280, 286, and 288.* Tony Stone Images: *pages 280, 282, and 284.*

... about Barbara Sestok

Barbara Sestok has compiled and been the key designer of the cross-stitch motifs you see in this book. She has been a designer in the needlework and fashion industry for 20 years. Barbara has worked in many mediums including crochet, stamped goods, paintings, latch hook, and counted cross-stitch. Cross-stitch is her favorite medium because, she says, "it is like painting with floss and needle."

Barbara grew up on the east side of Manhattan but always wanted to live in the country. Eighteen years ago she moved to the country where she lives with her family and many pets including a duck named Donald. She raises sheep and poultry and enjoys gardening, working with livestock, and creating designs that reflect the wide variety of nature around her that constantly inspires her to create her beautiful work.

stitchers

Mary Avaux
Russell Banker
Susan Banker
Kris Bryant
Betty Burlingame
Kolene DeLaney
Diana Dusing
Karen Eis
Nancy Eis
Susan Fiddler
Donna Glas
Cynthia Goodrich
Vicki Jacobs

Colleen Johnson
Gail Kimmel
Dana Kinnick
Carolyn Knittle
Joyce Koerner
Carla Munch
Tami Rupiper
Linda Rutz
Beth Sherman
Jennie Young